Student Book 1

Third Edition

Person to Person

Communicative Speaking and Listening Skills

Jack C. Richards   **David Bycina**   **Ingrid Wisniewska**

D1441590

OXFORD

UNIVERSITY PRESS

OXFORD
UNIVERSITY PRESS

198 Madison Avenue
New York, NY 10016 USA

Great Clarendon Street, Oxford OX2 6DP UK

Oxford University Press is a department of the University of Oxford.
It furthers the University's objective of excellence in research, scholarship,
and education by publishing worldwide in

Oxford New York

Auckland Cape Town Dar es Salaam Hong Kong Karachi
Kuala Lumpur Madrid Melbourne Mexico City Nairobi
New Delhi Shanghai Taipei Toronto

With offices in

Argentina Austria Brazil Chile Czech Republic France Greece
Guatemala Hungary Italy Japan Poland Portugal Singapore
South Korea Switzerland Thailand Turkey Ukraine Vietnam

OXFORD and OXFORD ENGLISH are registered trademarks of
Oxford University Press

© Oxford University Press 2005

Database right Oxford University Press (maker)

Library of Congress Cataloging-in-Publication Data

Richards, Jack C.
  Person to person : communicative speaking and listening skills / Jack
C. Richards, David Bycina, Ingrid Wisniewska.—3rd ed.
    p. cm.
  Contents: Student book 1–Student book 2.
  Rev. ed. of: New person to person student book. New York : Oxford University
Press, c1995–

  ISBN 978-0-19-430213-5 (student book 1)

  ISBN 978-0-19-430212-8 (student book 1 with CD)
  [etc.]
  1. English language—Textbooks for foreign speakers. 2. English language—
Spoken English—Problems, exercises, etc. 3. Oral communication—Problems,
exercises, etc. 4. Listening—Problems, exercises, etc. I. Bycina, David. II.
Wisniewska, Ingrid. III. Richards, Jack C. New person to person student book.
IV. Title.

PE1128.R46 2005
428.3'4-dc22

2004065481

No unauthorized photocopying

All rights reserved. No part of this publication may be reproduced,
stored in a retrieval system, or transmitted, in any form or by any means,
without the prior permission in writing of Oxford University Press,
or as expressly permitted by law, or under terms agreed with the appropriate
copyright clearance organization. Enquiries concerning reproduction outside
the scope of the above should be sent to the ELT Rights Department, Oxford
University Press, at the address above.

You must not circulate this book in any other binding or cover
and you must impose this same condition on any acquirer.

Any websites referred to in this publication are in the public domain and
their addresses are provided by Oxford University Press for information only.
Oxford University Press disclaims any responsibility for the content.

Executive Publisher: Nancy Leonhardt
Senior Acquisitions Editor: Chris Balderston
Senior Editor: Patricia O'Neill
Editor: Mike Boyle
Associate Editor: Amy E. Hawley
Assistant Editor: Kate Schubert
Art Director: Lynn Luchetti
Design Project Manager: Maj-Britt Hagsted
Senior Designer: Claudia Carlson
Art Editor: Elizabeth Blomster
Production Manager: Shanta Persaud
Production Controller: Zainaltu Jawat Ali

ISBN 978 0 19 430212 8

Printed in China

Printing (last digit): 10 9

This book is printed on paper from certified and well-managed sources.

ACKNOWLEDGMENTS

Consider This sections written by Lewis Lansford

Illustrations by: Gary Antonetti pp.33 (directions), 34, 52; Barbara Bastian pp.13,
35, 51, 65, 69, 95, 109, 111, 113, 115; Kathy Baxendale pp.23, 38, 43, 46, 57
(clothes), 63, 97, 110; Chris Costello pp.55, 61, 112; Martha Gavin pp.8 (people),
16, 27 (people), 45, 59, 78; Neil Gower pp.33 (map), 93, 94, 98 (brochure); Mike
Hortens pp.9 (ID cards), 26, 29, 47 (planner), 104, 106 (ID cards); Jon Keegan pp.5,
11, 39, 73 (people), 77, 114; Rob Kemp pp.30, 57 (chart), 87, 103; Eric Larsen
pp.19 (middle and bottom), 21 (top), 25, 82, 99, 108; Arnie Levin pp.44, 47
(cartoon), 71; Colin Mier pp.9 (illustration), 19 (top), 27 (room), 91, 106
(illustration); Karen Minot pp.8 (directory), 21 (bottom), 31, 42, 53, 64, 79, 85, 86;
Sandy Nichols pp.37, 41, 60, 72, 83, 101, 102, 105; Geo Parkin pp.3, 12, 17, 76,
107; Chris Robson pp.20, 24, 49, 73 (objects), 98 (pictures)

Cover photograph by: Dennis Kitchen Studio

Location and studio photography by: Dennis Kitchen Studio pp. 2, 6, 10, 14, 18, 22,
36, 40, 44, 48, 54, 58, 62, 66, 70, 74, 80, 84, 88, 92, 96, 100; Kjeld Duits pp. 28, 32

*The publishers would like to thank the following for their permission to reproduce
photographs.* Alamy: Ace Stock Limited p.95 (Carnival); allOver photography p.80
(moving day); AM Corporation p.95 (Cable car); Brand X Pictures p.20 (newspaper), 95 (skyscrapers), 115
(Honolulu beach, Bangkok temple); BananaStock p.90 (Golden Gate Bridge); Bob
Thomas p.90 (waterfront); Chad Ehlers p.89 (Tokyo); Dex Image p.15 (Asian man);
Digital Vision: Stewart Cohen p.9 (man); Dieter Melhorn p.115 (Honolulu beach);
Douglas Peebles p.115 (Luau); Dynamic Graphics Group/Creatas p.89 (Paris);
Dynamic Graphics Group/IT Stock Free p.106 (woman); Hideo Kurihara p.115
(volcano); Hemera Technologies p.20 (book); imageshop - zefa visual media uk ltd
p.90 (streetcars); Index Stock p.90 (Trans American); Ingram Publishing p.20
(telephone, disk); John Powell p.15 (Caucasian woman); mediacolor's p.95
(market); Medioimages p.95 (Hong Kong dhows); Mihai Florin p.88 (Russia); Pat
Behnke p.95 (Hong Kong waterfront), 115 (batik clothing); Peter Arnold, Inc. p.62
(rattlesnake); The Photolibrary Wales p.89 (Bangkok); Robert Harding Picture
Library Ltd. p.90 (old homes); RubberBall p.15 (man); Steve Skjold p.96 (volunteer
work); Sue Cunningham Photographic p.95 (Copacabana beach); Travel Ink p.115
(Bangkok food); Westend61 p.115 (night scene); Allsport Concepts: Marcus
Boesch p.70 (bobsled); Brand X Pictures: Burke/Triolo Productions p.20
(videotape); Corbis:Reuters p.86 (Sting); FoodPix: Brian Leatart p.43 (baklava);
Freedomship.com p.36 (Freedom floating city); Gosselin Family p.10 (sextuplets);
Harley Davidson p.28 (kids on bike); Image 100 p.26 (wedding photo); The Image
Bank: Barros&Barros p.15 (teen); Bernhard Lang p.9 (woman); Marc Romanelli
p.15 (African American woman); Richard Drury p.20 (calendar); Ron Krisel p.15
(Hispanic woman); National Geographic: Bruce Dale p.18 (microchip); Photodisc
Green: David Toase p.20 (scissors); C Squared Studios p.20 (eyeglasses); Stone:
Donald Nausbaum p.43 (Carnival); Silvestre Machado p.43 (Rio coastline), 95 (Rio
from above); Taxi: Justin Pumfrey p.43 (Thai jungle); Sigrid Olsson p.106 (man);
Travel Pix p.43 (Thai handicraft)

Special Thanks To: City University of New York Graduate Center, The New York
Public Library Science, Industry and Business Library

*The publishers would like to thank the following people for their help in developing this new
edition:* Laura MacGregor, Tokyo, Japan; Su-Wei Wang, Taiwan; and Max
Wollerton, Tokyo, Japan.

The publishers would like to thank the following OUP staff for their support and assistance:
Satoko Shimoyama, and Ted Yoshioka.

Welcome to *Person to Person*. Let's take a look at the sections of the units.

Conversations The two conversations present examples of the language you will be studying. You can listen to them on the CD in class or at home.

Give It a Try This section teaches the language points from the conversations. You will focus on each one separately and then practice them with a partner.

Listen to This The listening section gives you real-life listening tasks that help you review your understanding of the language from the unit. You answer questions or complete charts about the listening.

Let's Talk These are pair- or group-work activities that ask you to expand on what you have learned. You can use both the language you have learned and your imagination.

Consider This "Consider This" presents some interesting facts on a cultural topic related to the theme of the unit. You can use these facts as an introduction to the unit.

Pronunciation Focus A pronunciation point related to the language from the unit comes after Conversation 2. This helps you to practice the language in the unit in a more natural way.

Person to Person These pages present a problem based on the language from the unit. You and a partner will work together to solve the problem, using the language you have learned, as well as your own ideas and opinions.

In addition to the language presented in each unit, here are some expressions that will be very useful to you—both inside and outside of class.

1. Please say that again.
2. I'm sorry. I don't understand.
3. Please speak more slowly.
4. How do you say _____ in English?
5. What does _____ mean?
6. I don't know.
7. May I ask a question?
8. How do you spell _____?

We hope you find that learning to speak and understand English is easier than you think. Good luck!

Contents

Unit 1

Nice to meet you.   2

  1. Introducing yourself   3
  2. Getting the name right   3
  3. Asking someone's occupation   3
  4. Asking for more information   4

Could I have your name, please?   6

  1. Names   7
  2. Addresses   7
  3. Telephone and e-mail   7

Unit 2

Tell me about your family.   10

  1. Describing your family   11
  2. Marital status and children   11
  3. Talking about age   12

What does she look like?   14

  1. Asking about age   15
  2. Asking for a description   15
  3. Describing clothing   16

Unit 3

Do you know where it is?   18

  1. Asking where things are (informal)   19
  2. Asking where things are (formal)   19

What does it look like?   22

  1. Describing things (1)   23
  2. Describing things (2)   23
  3. Describing uses   24

Review: Units 1–3   26

Unit 4

See you then!   28

  1. Days and dates   29
  2. Starting and finishing times   29
  3. Opening and closing times   30

How do I get there?   32

  1. Describing locations   33
  2. Giving directions   33

Unit 5

How do you like the city?   36

  1. Talking about likes and dislikes   37

I love sight-seeing!   40

  1. Agreeing and disagreeing with likes and dislikes   41
  2. Stating preferences   42

Unit 6

How about coming with us?   44

  1. Accepting invitations   45
  2. Declining invitations   45
  3. Getting more information   46

Why don't we meet there?   48

  1. Suggesting another day   49
  2. Setting the time and place   49
  3. Changing plans   50
  4. Adding to plans   50

Review: Units 4–6   52

Unit 7

Could you help me?   54

  1. Getting and giving help   55
  2. Getting information   55
  3. Asking prices   56

This sweater is more stylish.   58

  1. Comparing things (1)   59
  2. Comparing things (2)   59
  3. Returning things   60

Unit 8

And what would you like?   62

  1. Discussing the menu   63
  2. Ordering   63
  3. Adding extra information to your order   64

Would you care for any dessert?   66

  1. Describing food   67
  2. Offering additional food or drink   67
  3. Offering other suggestions   68

Unit 9

Could I borrow that?   70

  1. Making small requests   71
  2. Making larger requests   71
  3. Asking for favors   72

Could you change my room?   74

  1. Complaining politely   75
  2. Requesting action or change   75
  3. Accepting an apology   76

Review: Units 7–9   78

Unit 10

Where are you from?   80

  1. Giving and getting personal information (1)   81
  2. Giving and getting personal information (2)   81
  3. Being specific   82

How long did you do that?   84

  1. Discussing length of time   85
  2. Asking *What next?*   85
  3. Describing changes   86

Unit 11

Have you ever been to Japan?   88

  1. Asking about past experiences   89
  2. Asking for a description or opinion   89
  3. Asking for more details   90

Which city did you like better?   92

  1. Comparing places (1)   93
  2. Comparing places (2)   93
  3. Comparing places (3)   94

Unit 12

What are you going to do?   96

  1. Discussing future plans (1)   97
  2. Discussing future plans (2)   97
  3. Discussing future plans (3)   98

What do you want to do?   100

  1. Discussing goals   101
  2. Discussing hopes   101
  3. Discussing possibilities   102

Review: Units 10–12   104

Person to Person Student B pages   106
Audio script   116

Conversation 1
Nice to meet you.

Where do you make friends and meet people? Make a list of places.

CONSIDER THIS

What's the world's most common last name?

張

Some say it's Zhang (sometimes written *Chang*). There are about 100 million Zhangs in the world.

- What's the meaning of your last name?
- Is your last name common in your home country?
- What's the meaning of your first name?

Class CD 1, Track 2

Pat:	The noodles look good. I think I'll try some of them.
Bo-wei:	Is the pizza good, too?
Pat:	Yeah, the pizza is usually very good. My name's Patricia by the way. Nice to meet you.
Bo-wei:	Sorry, what's your name again?
Pat:	Patricia. But please call me Pat.
Bo-wei:	Pat…I'm Bo-wei. So, what do you do?
Pat:	I'm studying medicine.
Bo-wei:	Really?
Pat:	Yeah. How about you?
Bo-wei:	I'm a computer programmer. But now I'm studying English.
Pat:	Oh, are you? That's great!
Bo-wei:	Yeah, it's fun.
Pat:	Oh, we'd better keep moving or we'll lose our place in line!

Student CD, Track 2

GIVE IT A TRY

1. Introducing yourself

| Hello. | My name's | Patricia. | Hello. | My name's | Bo-wei. |
| Hi. | I'm | | Hi. | I'm | |

PRACTICE

Class CD 1 Track 3 Listen to the example. Then introduce yourself to your classmates.

2. Getting the name right

Sorry, what's your	name	again?	(It's) Patricia, but please call me Pat.
	first name		(It's) Patricia Johnson, but please call me Patricia.
	last name		
Sorry, I didn't catch / get your name.			

PRACTICE

Class CD 1 Track 4 Listen to the example. Then introduce yourself to other classmates. This time, ask the person to repeat his or her first name or last name.

3. Asking someone's occupation

What do you do?	I'm	studying medicine.
		a computer programmer.
Really? Oh, are you? That's great!	Yeah. How about you?	

PRACTICE

Class CD 1 Track 5 Listen to the example. Then ask your classmates their occupations.

Unit 1 **3**

4. Asking for more information

A: What do you do?

B: I'm a student.
A: Really? What school do you go to?
B: (I go to) | McGill University.
             | Boston College.
A: What are you studying?
B: (I'm studying) | graphic design.
                  | medicine.

medicine	art	computer science
English	music	graphic design
economics	fashion	

B: I'm an engineer.
A: Really? What company do you work for?
B: I work for | a computer company.
              | Digital Electronics.
A: What do you do there exactly?
B: I'm | a designer.
       | in the sales department.

architect	artist	musician
journalist	designer	photographer
actor	chef	

PRACTICE

Class CD 1 Track 6 Listen to the example. Then interview your partner and find out what he or she does. Use the words in the chart.

LISTEN TO THIS

Class CD 1 Track 7 *Part 1* Listen to three conversations and decide where the people are. Number them in the correct order.

___ film festival   ___ conference   ___ wedding   ___ graduation   ___ party

Part 2 Listen to the conversations again and complete the information below.

Conversation 1			
Man's name:	Bradley	Woman's name:	Owens
Occupation:		Occupation:	

Conversation 2			
Man's name:	Hunt	Woman's name:	Lee
He studies:		She studies:	
His school:		Her school:	

Conversation 3			
Man's name:	Pirelli	Woman's name:	Sato
His occupation:		She studies:	
His company:		Her school:	

Part 3 Which conversation starter was the best? Why?

LET'S TALK

Part 1 Think of an occupation that you like. Write it on a piece of paper. Give the paper to your teacher or group leader. Your teacher will fold up the papers and give you a different piece of paper.

Part 2 Walk around the room and ask questions to find out what your job is. You can only ask Yes / No questions. You can only ask each person one question. When you guess your job, help the other students.

Part 3 Now imagine you are all at a party. Walk around the room and introduce yourself and your new job. Ask questions to find out about other students' jobs. Try to talk to everyone in the room.

Part 4 Who does what? How many jobs can you remember? Make a list.

Conversation 2
Could I have your name, please?

Where do you usually have to give your name and address? Make a list of places.

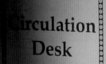

Class CD 1, Track 8

Librarian:	Yes, can I help you?
Bo-wei:	I'd like to get a library card, please.
Librarian:	Certainly. First I'll need some information from you. Could I have your name, please?
Bo-wei:	It's Bo-wei. Bo-wei Zhang.
Librarian:	And how do you spell your last name?
Bo-wei:	It's Z-h-a-n-g.
Librarian:	Thank you. Could I please have your address, Mr. Zhang?
Bo-wei:	2418 Graystone Road.
Librarian:	Is that in New York?
Bo-wei:	Yes, that's right. The zip code is 11211.
Librarian:	OK, and please give me your telephone number.
Bo-wei:	It's 917-555-9758.
Librarian:	917-555-9758. All right. Do you have an e-mail address?
Bo-wei:	Yes, it's bowei33@internet.com.
Librarian:	Are you a student?
Bo-wei:	Yes, I'm studying English.
Librarian:	Fine, I just need an ID card and we'll be all set.

Class CD 1, Track 9
Pronunciation Focus

In compound nouns, the first noun is stressed more than the second noun.

LIBRARY card   **TELEPHONE** number
LAST name   **E-MAIL** address
ZIP code   **ID** card

Listen to the conversation again and notice the stress in compound nouns.

Student CD, Track 3

GIVE IT A TRY

1. Names

Could I have your name, please?		It's Bo-wei. Bo-wei Zhang.
How do you spell your	first | name? last |	It's | B-o (dash) w-e-i. Z-h-a-n-g.

PRACTICE 1

Class CD 1 Track 10

Listen to the example. Then ask your partner his or her name and how to spell it.

PRACTICE 2

Repeat Practice 1 with three other classmates.

2. Addresses

Where do you live? Could I have your address?	I live at 2418 Graystone Road. My address is 2418 Graystone Road.
Is that in New York?	Yes, that's right. No, it's in New Jersey.

PRACTICE 1

Class CD 1 Track 11

Listen to the example. Then ask your partner the name of his or her street and how to spell it. Confirm the city.

PRACTICE 2

Repeat Practice 1 with three other classmates.

> **◎ Use These Words**
>
> Street names in the U.S. and Canada:
>
> Rd. = Road   St. = Street
 Ave. = Avenue   Dr. = Drive
 Blvd. = Boulevard

3. Telephone and e-mail

What's your telephone number? Please give me your e-mail address.	(It's) | 917-555-9758. bowei33@internet.com.

PRACTICE 1

Class CD 1 Track 12

Listen to the example. Then ask your partner his or her telephone number. Repeat it and write it down. Ask for his or her e-mail address.

PRACTICE 2

Repeat Practice 1 with three other classmates. Make a list.

Class CD 1
Track 13

Listen to the example. Student A is the operator. Student B calls the operator to ask for the number of one of the people on the list below. Reverse roles.

A: Directory Assistance. What city, please?
B: New York. I'd like the number of Amanda Rhodes.
A: How do you spell the last name, please?
B: It's R-h-o-d-e-s.
A: Thank you. And could I have the address?
B: It's 418 South Street.
A: The number is 718-987-0248.
B: 718-987-0248. Thank you very much.
A: You're welcome.

Abel, David 724 Eastern Ave........ 718-867-5307
Abel, Debbie 9 Woodgate Rd........ 718-455-4433
Chan, Amy 12 Lakeside Place...... 718-896-3427
Mo, Alex 845 Cherry St.............. 718-211-3952
Park, Dana 1989 River St............ 718-227-5486
Park, Sun-Woo 18 Palmgrove Blvd. 718-987-2718
Shimizu, Yoko 784 Kingston Rd..... 718-555-1690

LISTEN TO THIS

Class CD 1
Track 14

Part 1 Listen to the conversation between a customer and a salesperson. What is the customer applying for? Which of the following does the salesperson ask for? Number them in the correct order as you hear them.

___ city   ___ home phone   ___ e-mail address   _1_ name
___ zip code   ___ street address   ___ work phone   ___ occupation

Part 2 Listen to the conversation again and fill out the form.

Lacy's **Department Store**   *Credit Card Application*

First Name_____ Last Name_____
Home Telephone_____ Work Telephone_____
Address_____
City_____ State *Massachusetts* Zip Code_____
E-mail Address_____
Occupation_____
Employer_____

Part 3 How is this application form different from applications you have filled out recently?

(Students A and B look at this page. Students C and D look at page 106.)

Part 1 Students A and B will interview Students C and D together. Complete the missing information for Students C and D.

Student A: You are Ming Chen.

Student B: You are Chris Brown.

IDENTIFICATION	IDENTIFICATION
First Name: **Ming**	First Name: **Chris**
Last Name: **Chen**	Last Name: **Brown**
Street Address: **60 Carpenter Street**	Street Address: **218 Darmouth Avenue**
City: **San Francisco, California, U.S.**	City: **Sydney, Australia**
Zip code: **94103**	Zip code: **NSW 2006**
Telephone: **415-497-5003**	Telephone: **3602-1876**
Occupation: **computer programmer**	Occupation: **medical student**
A765Z10 E-mail: **chenming@coolmail.com**	J345L05 E-mail: **cbrown77@sharemail.com**

Write Student C's information here:

Write Student D's information here:

IDENTIFICATION	IDENTIFICATION
First Name: _____	First Name: _____
Last Name: _____	Last Name: _____
Street Address: _____	Street Address: _____
City: _____	City: _____
Zip code: _____	Zip code: _____
Telephone: _____	Telephone: _____
Occupation: _____	Occupation: _____
E-mail: _____	E-mail: _____

Part 2 Now show your page to Students C and D. Is all the information the same? Ask questions to check spelling.

Part 3 Imagine all four of you are at a party. Introduce yourselves to each other. Say your name, where you live, and what you do.

Now Try This

Walk around the class and introduce yourself again. use your own personal information. Make a list of everyone you meet with all their information.

Conversation 1
Tell me about your family.

How many people are in your family? Do you prefer small families or big families?

CONSIDER THIS

Do you have any brothers or sisters?

Joel Gosselin has two brothers and three sisters—and all six children were born on May 11, 2004! They're sextuplets! The chance of having two babies (or twins) is 1 in 89!

Babies	Chances
three	1 in 7,921
four	1 in 704,969
five	1 in 62,742,241
six	1 in 5,584,059,449

- Do you know any twins?
- Would you like to have five brothers or sisters?

Class CD 1, Track 15

Niki:	I love that new T-shirt you're wearing!
Liana:	Thanks! My sister gave it to me for my birthday.
Niki:	She has good taste. How old is she?
Liana:	Actually, she's the same age as me, 24. We're twins. Look, here's a photo of us together.
Niki:	Wow, you really look alike! And who's that?
Liana:	That's my brother, Joseph. He's a musician.
Niki:	Is he married?
Liana:	Yes, he is. And he has two children, Anna and Max.
Niki:	You look too young to be an aunt! Do they live near you?
Liana:	No, they live far away, but they're coming here to visit soon. I can't wait to see them again. So, tell me about your family. Do you have any brothers or sisters?
Niki:	Yes, I have three brothers, but no sisters. They're all younger than me. I'm the oldest.

GIVE IT A TRY

1. Describing your family

| Tell me about your family. | | |
| Do you have | any brothers or sisters? | |
Have you got		
I have	three brothers	but no sisters.
I've got		and one sister.
No, I'm an only child.		
We're twins.		

Use These Words

grandmother	grandfather
mother	father
daughter	son
sister	brother
sister-in-law	brother-in-law
aunt	uncle
niece	nephew
cousin	cousin

PRACTICE 1

Class CD 1
Track 16

Listen to the example. Ask your partner if he or she has any brothers or sisters.

PRACTICE 2

Look at the family tree. Student A is Amy. Student B asks about her family.

PRACTICE 3

Describe your family to your partner. Your partner will draw your family tree.

2. Marital status and children

| Is your brother / sister married? | Yes, he / she is. |
Is he / she single?	No, he / she isn't. He's / she's married / single.
Does he / she have any children?	Yes, he / she has two children.
	No, he / she doesn't.

PRACTICE

Class CD 1
Track 17

Listen to the example. Then ask your classmates about their families.

3. Talking about age

How old is your sister / brother?	She's 24.
	She's the same age as me.
	We're the same age.
How old are your brothers / sisters?	The oldest is 40.
	The middle one is 32.
	The youngest is 16.
Are you the oldest / youngest?	Yes, I am.
	No, I'm the youngest.

PRACTICE

Class CD 1
Track 18

Listen to the example. Then ask your partner about the ages of his or her brothers or sisters. (If he or she is an only child, ask about cousins.) Reverse roles. Then ask another classmate.

LISTEN TO THIS

Part 1 Look at the pictures. What do you think is happening in each one? What do you think the family relationships are?

Class CD 1
Track 19

Part 2 Listen to Claire talking about her 21st birthday party. Number the pictures 1–4.

Part 3 Describe Claire's family to your partner. Draw her family tree.

Part 1 You are going to do a class survey. First, read the chart in Part 3 and put a check (✔) in every box that's true for you.

Part 2 Write down three questions you will ask your classmates to find out how many brothers and sisters they have.

1. _____

2. _____

3. _____

Part 3 Ask everyone your questions. Mark the chart with their answers. Remember to make a note of which students you have asked.

Class Survey

	1	2	3	4+	Student Names
Younger brothers					
Older brothers					
Younger sisters					
Older sisters					
Total brothers and sisters					
Oldest child					
Youngest child					
Only child					

Part 4 Compare your answers by making sentences about your chart.

Example: Three people in the class have no brothers or sisters.

Conversation 2
What does she look like?

Describe the two people in the picture. Include their age, clothing, and appearance.

Class CD 1, Track 20

Niki: Hi, Jack! You're in Liana's class, aren't you? Could you give this to her for me? She's already in class, and I have to run.

Jack: Sure, no problem. But what does Liana look like? Is she the girl with really short curly hair and long earrings?

Niki: Oh, you don't know Liana! Do you see the girl sitting right at the back of the class? She's pretty short, and slim, in her mid-twenties. She has long black hair.

Jack: Hmm. I don't see anyone like that. What's she wearing?

Niki: She's wearing a black T-shirt.

Jack: Oh yes, I see her. I'll give this to her, no problem.

Niki: Thanks!

Student CD, Track 5

Class CD 1, Track 21
Pronunciation Focus

In spoken English, words are often linked together. Listen to the first two words of these sentences.

Could you give this to Liana?

What does Liana look like?

Is she the girl with short hair?

Listen to the conversation again and notice the linked words.

GIVE IT A TRY

1. Asking about age

How old is	she?	Pretty	young.	She's in her early teens.
	he?	Kind of	old.	He's in his mid-twenties.
How old are they?		Middle-aged. They're in their late forties.		

Class CD 1
Track 22

PRACTICE 1

Listen to the example. Then choose one of the pictures below. Describe the person's age. Your partner will guess who you are describing.

A: She's pretty young. She's in her early twenties.
B: That's Vicky.

Vicky

Samira

Tony

Mike

Dexter

Pauline

PRACTICE 2

Ask your partner the ages of three famous people. Reverse roles.

2. Asking for a description

What does he / she look like? What do they look like?	He's fairly tall / short. She's pretty slim / heavy. They're kind of tall and thin.
What color is his / her hair?	It's blonde / black / gray. He has brown / red / gray hair. He's bald.
What's his / her hair like?	It's long / short / medium length. It's straight / wavy / curly. She has long curly hair.

PRACTICE

Class CD 1
Track 23

Listen to the example. Then look at the pictures from Practice 1. Describe one of them to your partner. Your partner will guess who you are describing. Reverse roles.

A: She has shoulder length, wavy brown hair.
B: That's Vicky.

3. Describing clothing

What is he / she wearing?	He's wearing	jeans and a blue T-shirt.
What are they wearing?	She's wearing	black pants and a green sports shirt.
What does he / she have on?	They're wearing	a black skirt and a red top.
What do they have on?		a navy blue uniform.
		raincoats.

He has a brown jacket on.
She has a red skirt on.
They have winter clothes on.

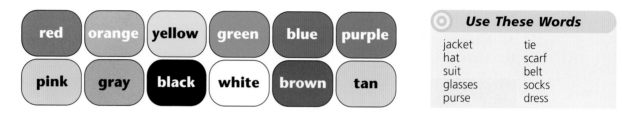

red orange yellow green blue purple
pink gray black white brown tan

🎯 Use These Words

jacket	tie
hat	scarf
suit	belt
glasses	socks
purse	dress

PRACTICE

Choose one of the people below and describe his or her clothing to your partner.

LISTEN TO THIS

Part 1 Three people saw a man driving a motorcycle through the flower garden at City Hall. A police officer is asking about his description. What questions do you think he will ask?

Class CD 1
Track 24

Part 2 Listen to three different people describing the man. Fill in the chart below.

	Height	Weight	Age	Hair	Clothing
1					
2					
3					

Part 3 What do you think the man looked like?

(Student A looks at this page. Student B looks at page 107.)

Part 1 Look at Ann's family tree. Look at each family member and think of how you can describe each person's age, appearance, hair, clothing, and family relationship.

Part 2 Your partner also has a family tree. There are ten differences between the two family trees. Ask questions to find the differences. Don't look at your partner's page.

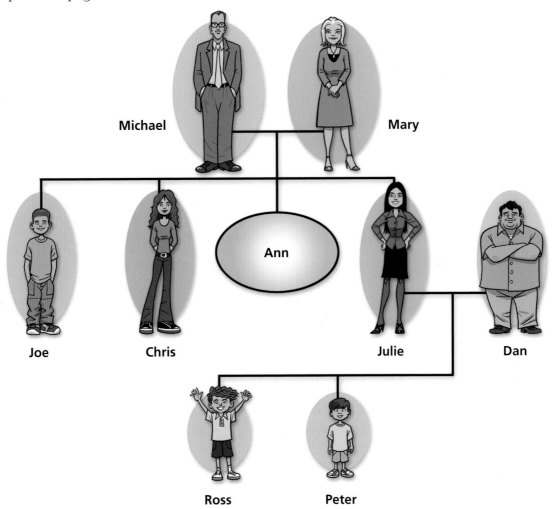

Part 3 Write sentences about the differences between the two family trees.

Example: My tree has one younger brother, but my partner's tree has…

Now Try This

Write sentences about the differences between your family and your partner's family.

Conversation 1
Do you know where it is?

How many things in the store can you name? Make a list. Add your own words.

CONSIDER THIS

Where's the dog?

Some people put a tiny computer chip under their pet's skin. It carries information—for example, name and address—that can help if the pet is lost.

● Some experts say that people will soon have tiny chips in their bodies, too. Do you think this is a good idea?
● Have you ever been lost? Where? What happened?

Class CD 1, Track 25

Marlene:	Hi! What are you doing here?
Jung-soo:	Buying school supplies. I need some binders.
Marlene:	I'm out of paper! Where's the copy paper?
Jung-soo:	I think it's in this aisle, on the top shelf, to the right of the computer disks.
Marlene:	Oh, yes, I see it.
Jung-soo:	Do you know where the binders are?
Marlene:	Yeah, they're on the middle shelf, next to the paper clips.
Jung-soo:	Great! I need those, too.
Marlene:	It looks like you're going to be busy!

Student CD, Track 6

GIVE IT A TRY

1. Asking where things are (informal)

| Where | is the copy paper?
are the binders? | It's
They're | on
above | the shelf.
the notebooks. |

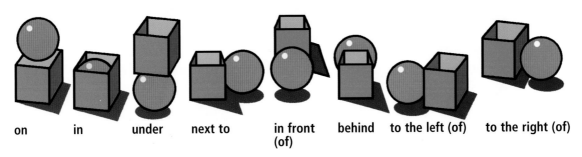

on   in   under   next to   in front (of)   behind   to the left (of)   to the right (of)

PRACTICE

Class CD 1 Track 26

Listen to the example. You are at a friend's home helping them with their homework. Ask your friend about the following things. Reverse roles.

Student A
copy paper
printer
pencils
newspaper
pens
computer disks

Student B
wastebasket
self-stick notes
calculator
notebooks
headphones
cell phone

2. Asking where things are (formal)

| Do you know where | my notebook is?
my computer disks are? |
| It's
They're | on the top shelf between the printer and the paper.
in the corner behind the wastebasket. |

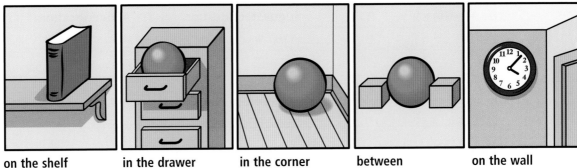

on the shelf   in the drawer   in the corner   between   on the wall

**Class CD 1
Track 27**

Listen to the example. Then ask where things are. Reverse roles. Continue asking about other items.

Use These Words

dictionary	paper clips
binder	copy paper
files	calendar
self-stick notes	stapler
CDs	coffee

LISTEN TO THIS

**Class CD 1
Track 28**

Part 1 Listen to four short conversations. Which of these objects are the speakers looking for? Write the correct number next to each one.

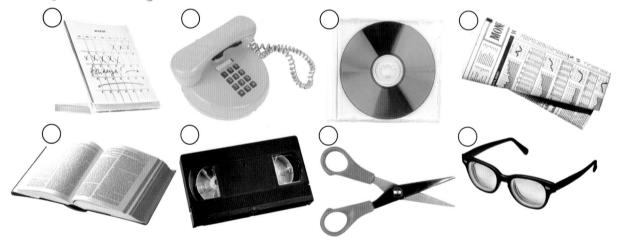

Part 2 Listen again and complete the chart.

	Object	Suggested location	Actual location
1		*In the desk drawer.*	
2			*Under the newspaper.*
3			
4			

Part 3 Describe the location of each object.

Part 1 Below is a picture of your office. Decide where you will put all the items in your office by writing the letters on the picture.

a. paper   b. phone book   c. dictionary   d. pencils   e. CDs

f. phone   g. computer disks   h. calculator   i. headphones   j. notebooks

Part 2 Ask questions to find out where things are in student B's office and write the correct letter on student B's picture. Then compare your answers. Reverse roles.

Part 3 Make a list of ten objects in your desk space at home or at work. Describe where they are to your partner. Your partner will draw your desk space. Reverse roles.

Write a list of 10 objects here: Draw your partner's desk:

1. _____
2. _____
3. _____
4. _____
5. _____
6. _____
7. _____
8. _____
9. _____
10. _____

Conversation 2
What does it look like?

How many things in the office can you name? Where are they located?

Class CD 1, Track 29

Fu-an: Marlene…? I can't find the what-do-you-call-it.

Marlene: What can't you find?

Fu-an: You know. The thing for…oh, it's on the tip of my tongue!

Marlene: What does it look like? Maybe I can help you find it.

Fu-an: It's a long, narrow, flat thing made of plastic.

Marlene: OK. What color is it, and what's it used for?

Fu-an: It's green, and you use it for drawing straight lines.

Marlene: Fu-an! You mean a ruler! It's in the box next to the telephone.

Fu-an: Oh, yeah, ruler! That's what it's called! Thanks, Marlene. I don't know what's wrong with me today.

Student CD, Track 7

Class CD 1, Track 30
Pronunciation Focus

Words ending in a consonant sound are often linked to words beginning with a vowel sound.

it's in   made of

tip of   color is

Listen to the conversation again and notice the linked words.

GIVE IT A TRY

1. Describing things (1)

What size is it?	It's	big / small. long / short / tall. narrow / wide.
What shape is it?	It's	round / square / oval. rectangular / triangular. pointed / flat / thin.
What does it look like?		It's a long, narrow, flat thing.

PRACTICE

Class CD 1
Track 31

Listen to the example. Then choose one of the boxes below. Describe it to your partner. Your partner will guess which one you are describing.

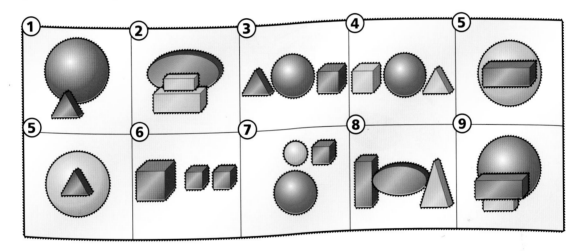

2. Describing things (2)

What's it What are they	made of?	It's They're	made of	wood. metal.

PRACTICE 1

Work in pairs. Make a list with as many objects as you can think of.

Objects made of:	
Wood:	Glass:
Plastic:	Paper:
Metal:	Leather:

PRACTICE 2

Choose one object from your list. Tell your partner what it's made of and what shape it is, but don't say what it is. Let your partner guess.

3. Describing uses

| What | is it
are they | used for? | It's used for opening doors.
You use them for cutting paper. |

PRACTICE

Class CD 1
Track 32 Listen to the example. Then choose one of the objects below and describe it for your partner to guess. Reverse roles.

A: It's small and thin and it's made of metal.
B: What's it used for?
A: It's used for opening doors.
B: It's a key.

LISTEN TO THIS

Part 1 Think of five inventions that have changed our lives. Make a list.

Class CD 1
Track 33 *Part 2* Listen to people describing inventions. Write the name of each object.

1	4
2	5
3	6

Part 3 Which of the inventions do you think is the most useful? Why?

(Student A looks at this page. Student B looks at page 108.)

Part 1 Look at the picture. Do you know what these inventions are for? How can you describe each one?

Part 2 Describe your four inventions to your partner. Where is the object? What does it look like? Your partner will draw the object on his or her picture and try to guess what it is used for. Reverse roles. (Remember: Don't say the name of the object or what it is used for. Your partner will guess.)

CD tower
scanner
answering machine
shredder

Now Try This

Think of a new gadget (a real or imaginary one!) for your home or for your office. What does it look like? What is it used for? Describe it to your partner. Your partner will try to guess what it is.

Review:
Units 1–3

LISTEN TO THIS UNIT 1

Class CD 1
Track 34

Part 1 You will hear a conversation between a bank manager and a new customer. Listen and write the information on the form.

SAVINGS ACCOUNT APPLICATION FORM

Name Mr. / Mrs. / Ms.

First _____ Last _____

HOME ADDRESS

Street _____

City _____ State _____ Zip Code _____

Phone _____

Occupation _____

Place of work _____

E-mail address _____

Part 2 Ask your partner questions to find out if your answers are the same.

GIVE IT A TRY

Part 1 Choose a famous person. Fill in the chart below.

Name	Address	Occupation	Place of work

Part 2 Walk around the room. Ask other students for their address, occupation, and place of work. (Don't ask for the name.) Try to guess who they are!

LISTEN TO THIS UNIT 2

Class CD 1
Track 35

Part 1 Nora went to her friend's wedding. Listen to her description of the photo. Which one is Nora? What are the names of Henry's mother and father? Write the name of each person on the photo.

Bob, Henry, Justin, Gina, Stephanie, Gemma, Eileen, Dan, Nora

Part 2 Imagine you are Nora. Describe your relationships to the other people.

Choose one of the people below. Describe the age, appearance, and clothing of your person. Include **one** detail that is incorrect. Your partner will try to guess which person you are describing and which detail is incorrect. Then reverse roles.

LISTEN TO THIS UNIT 3

Class CD 1
Track 36

Part 1 Listen to Edgar describe the following things in his workspace. What is he describing? Write the correct number next to each thing.

___ computer   ___ notebooks
___ wastebasket   ___ clock
___ rug   ___ calendar
___ plant   ___ dictionary
___ telephone   ___ binder

Part 2 Take turns describing things in the picture. Give just one clue at first. Then add more clues. Your partner will try to guess which thing you are describing.

GIVE IT A TRY

Do you have an idea for a new invention? Work in groups. Each person will describe his or her new invention to the group. What does it look like? What is it made of? What is it used for? Take a vote on the best invention. Draw a picture of the invention and show it to the class. Can they guess what it is for?

Conversation 1
See you then!

What kind of cultural events do you like to go to? What time do they usually start and finish?

CONSIDER THIS

Birthday party!

10,000 bikes + 50 exhibits + 25 bands = one big party!

The first Harley-Davidson motorcycle was built in 1903. In 2003, Harley-Davidson celebrated its 100th birthday in the U.S.A., and all over the world.

- Have you ever attended a big festival or celebration?
- How did you celebrate?

Class CD 1, Track 37

Vanessa: Kazu, is it your birthday this weekend?
Kazu: Yeah, it's this Saturday, the 28th.
Vanessa: Are you doing anything to celebrate? How about going to the music festival at Sun City Stadium? I can get you a ticket if you want.
Kazu: Really? That sounds great! What time does it start?
Vanessa: It starts at 4:00.
Kazu: Hmm…I'm afraid I can't make it by then. I have to study late on Saturday. What time does it end?
Vanessa: Not too late. Probably around 7:30. How about going to the Vienna Cafe for some cake and coffee after the concert?
Kazu: What time does the cafe close?
Vanessa: At midnight. Come on…you know it's a great idea.
Kazu: OK, Vanessa! I'll be there around 8:00. See you then!

Student CD, Track 8

1. Days and dates

When is	your birthday?	It's	on Monday.
When's	your anniversary?		in October.
	the party?		on October twenty-fourth.

PRACTICE

Class CD 1
Track 38

Listen to the example. Then walk around the class. Ask questions to find out when your classmates' birthdays are. Do any of your classmates share the same birthday?

2. Starting and finishing times

When	does it start?	It starts at	eight.
What time	does it end?	It ends around	eight o'clock.
			eight P.M.
			ten thirty.
			ten thirty P.M.
			half past ten.

PRACTICE

Class CD 1
Track 39

Listen to the example. Then read the events section from the Internet. Choose three different events (a movie, a play, a sports event), and ask your partner when they start and end. Reverse roles.

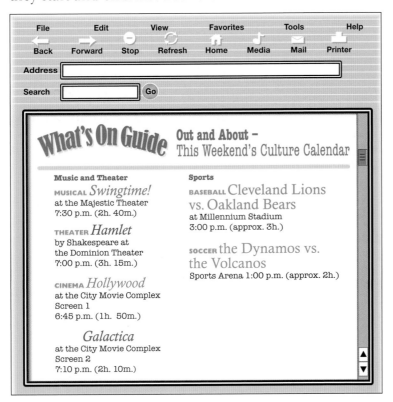

What's On Guide
Out and About –
This Weekend's Culture Calendar

Music and Theater

MUSICAL *Swingtime!*
at the Majestic Theater
7:30 p.m. (2h. 40m.)

THEATER *Hamlet*
by Shakespeare at
the Dominion Theater
7:00 p.m. (3h. 15m.)

CINEMA *Hollywood*
at the City Movie Complex
Screen 1
6:45 p.m. (1h. 50m.)

Galactica
at the City Movie Complex
Screen 2
7:10 p.m. (2h. 10m.)

Sports

BASEBALL Cleveland Lions
vs. Oakland Bears
at Millennium Stadium
3:00 p.m. (approx. 3h.)

SOCCER the Dynamos vs.
the Volcanos
Sports Arena 1:00 p.m. (approx. 2h.)

3. Opening and closing times

Could you	(please) tell me	when	you open?
Can you		what time	you close?

PRACTICE

Class CD 1
Track 40 Listen to the example. Then call the places below to find out their opening and closing times. Reverse roles.

A: Post office. Can I help you?
B: Hello. Could you please tell me when you open?
A: We open at 9:00 A.M.
B: And what time do you close?
A: At 5:30 P.M.
B: Thank you.
A: You're welcome.

OPENING AND CLOSING TIMES

POST OFFICE	9:00 A.M. TO 5:30 P.M.
BANK	9:00 A.M. TO 3:30 P.M.
MEDICAL CLINIC	9:00 A.M. TO 8:00 P.M.
MUSEUM OF MODERN ART	11:00 A.M. TO 6:00 P.M.
DRUGSTORE	10:00 A.M. TO 7:00 P.M.
LACY'S DEPARTMENT STORE	10:00 A.M. TO 9:30 P.M.

LISTEN TO THIS

Class CD 1
Track 41 *Part 1* Listen to information about three different places or events. Number them below in the correct order.

___ golf club   ___ music festival
___ swimming pool   ___ art gallery
___ movie theater   ___ rock concert

Part 2 Write the names of the places and events in the chart. Then listen again and fill in the missing information.

Place	Event	Times	Extra information
1			
2	1		
	2		
3			

Part 3 Where and when did each event take place?

Part 1 Work in groups. Each person in the group writes the opening and closing times for three places in the chart. Add any extra information, for example, *Closed on Sundays.*

Student A:
post office
bank
library

Student B:
pharmacy
video store
copy shop

Student C:
medical clinic
supermarket
Internet cafe

Part 2 Complete the rest of the chart by asking the other members of your group about opening and closing times. Add any helpful extra information.

	Place	Opening Time	Closing Time	Extra Information
1.				
2.				
3.				
4.				
5.				
6.				
7.				
8.				
9.				

Part 3 In your group, make a list of places that you wish would always stay open. Share your list with the class.

Conversation 2
How do I get there?

What do you do if you get lost? Think of three or four ways of finding your way.

Class CD 1, Track 42

Vanessa: Excuse me. Do you know where the Vienna Cafe is?

Man: No, I'm sorry. I don't speak English well.

Vanessa: OK, thanks anyway.

Vanessa: Excuse me. Which way is the Vienna Cafe?

Woman: Go straight for about three blocks. When you get to the subway station, turn left. It's next to the Megastore.

Vanessa: OK. Go up this street and turn left at the subway station. It's beside the Megastore.

Woman: That's it.

Vanessa: Thanks.

Woman: No problem.

Student CD, Track 9

Class CD 1, Track 43
Pronunciation Focus

Listen to the [w] sounds in the conversation. The [w] sound is often used to link words ending in the [o] sound to the next word.

How do I get there?

No, I'm sorry.

Go up this street.

Listen to the conversation again and mark the [w] sounds.

GIVE IT A TRY

1. Describing locations

Excuse me.	Do you know where the post office is?
	Could you tell me where the post office is?

Sure. It's on Elm Street,	across from the hardware store.
	between Eleventh and Twelfth Avenue.

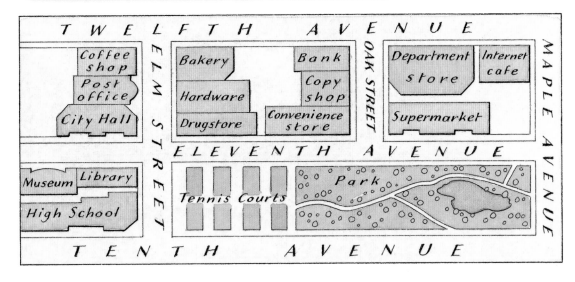

PRACTICE

Class CD 1
Track 44

Listen to the example. Then ask your partner about the location of these places on the map. If you can't find the place, say that you don't know where it is. Reverse roles.

Student A asks about

1. post office   3. camera store
2. copy shop   4. Internet cafe

Student B asks about

1. supermarket   3. library
2. video store   4. park

2. Giving directions

Excuse me.	Which way is the camera store?	It's	up / down this street on the right.
	How do I get to the park from here?		just past the bank.
		Go up	two blocks and turn right.
			this street and take the second left.

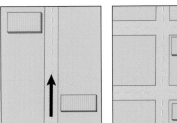 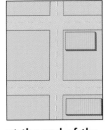 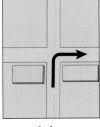 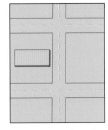 

up / down this street on the left   **at the end of the (next) block**   **around the corner on the right**   **in the middle of the block**   **(just) past**

PRACTICE 1

Class CD 1
Track 45

Listen to the example. Then look at the map below. Ask your partner how to get to the following places. Reverse roles. Student A starts from location A (stadium). Student B starts from location B (bus station).

Student A wants to get to
1. Jack's Cameras
2. Sam's Fitness Gym
3. Spin Music Store
4. Ace Video Rental

Student B wants to get to
1. Bill's Convenience Store
2. Spirit Clothing
3. Victor's Bookstore
4. Chinese Garden Restaurant

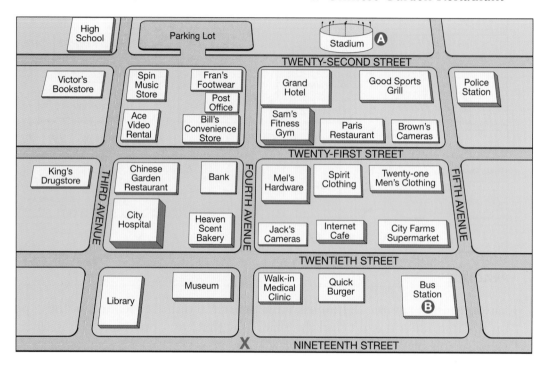

PRACTICE 2

Class CD 1
Track 46

Listen to the example. You are at point ✗ on the map. Take turns asking your partner where you can do these things. Reverse roles.

1. get some cash
2. eat lunch
3. send an e-mail
4. buy some aspirin
5. get some film
6. buy some stamps
7. see a doctor
8. buy some batteries

LISTEN TO THIS

Class CD 1
Track 47

Part 1 Listen to the conversations. Start at point ✗ on the map above and follow the directions by drawing a line. Then write down where each person is going.

1		3	
2		4	

Part 2 Describe the location of each place in Part 1.

Part 3 Choose a different starting point on the map. Describe the route to another place on the map. Your partner will guess the name of the place.

(Student A looks at this page. Student B looks at page 109.)

Part 1 Look at your map. Which buildings aren't labeled? Write two questions about them and then ask your partner.

1. _____

2. _____

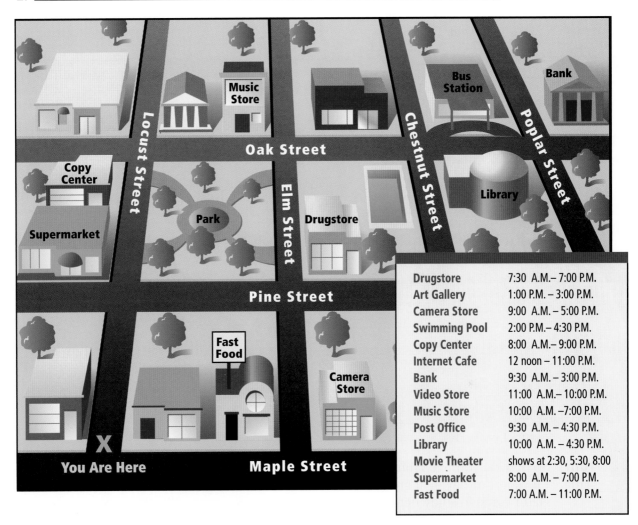

Drugstore	7:30 A.M.– 7:00 P.M.
Art Gallery	1:00 P.M. – 3:00 P.M.
Camera Store	9:00 A.M. – 5:00 P.M.
Swimming Pool	2:00 P.M.– 4:30 P.M.
Copy Center	8:00 A.M. – 9:00 P.M.
Internet Cafe	12 noon – 11:00 P.M.
Bank	9:30 A.M. – 3:00 P.M.
Video Store	11:00 A.M.– 10:00 P.M.
Music Store	10:00 A.M. –7:00 P.M.
Post Office	9:30 A.M. – 4:30 P.M.
Library	10:00 A.M. – 4:30 P.M.
Movie Theater	shows at 2:30, 5:30, 8:00
Supermarket	8:00 A.M. – 7:00 P.M.
Fast Food	7:00 A.M. – 11:00 P.M.

Part 2 This is your list of errands for tomorrow. Discuss your route on the map with your partner. Number the places on the map in the order that you visit them, and write the time next to each one. Remember to allow time for each errand.

get some cash
get some medicine
get your photos developed
buy a CD
borrow a book on English grammar

(together with your partner)
have lunch
see a movie
go swimming

Now Try This

Draw an X somewhere on your map. That is your home. Tell your partner how to get there from another point on the map. Your partner will tell you how to get to his or her home from your home. Then compare maps.

Conversation 1
How do you like the city?

What do you like about big cities?
What do you dislike?

CONSIDER THIS

A new kind of city

Name: Freedom
Population: 50,000 residents
   4,000 businesses
   15,000 employees
Location: The ocean, circling
   the world once every three
   years
Size: Over 1 kilometer long,
   230 meters wide, and
   25 stories tall
Services: Doctors, fitness clubs,
   restaurants, etc.
Tax: None

- Would you like to live in
  Freedom? Why or why not?

Class CD 1, Track 48

Amy: So how do you like Hong Kong?
Tina: I love it! I'm having a great time. I'm so glad I came to study here. What do you think of Hong Kong?
Amy: I love the stores and shopping for clothes!
Tina: I like the cultural events, too—all the concerts and art shows.
Amy: But the traffic is pretty bad.
Tina: Yeah. I hate all the traffic. It's really noisy. But every large city has traffic, you know?
Amy: Listen, it's almost lunchtime. There are lots of restaurants around here. What kind of food do you want to eat? Vietnamese? Thai? Italian? Mexican?
Tina: I can't stand making decisions. You choose!
Amy: OK. Let's have Vietnamese! We can have vegetarian dumplings and ban hoi!

Student CD, Track 10

GIVE IT A TRY

1. Talking about likes and dislikes

How do you like	the city?	I love it / them.
What do you think of	the people?	I really like it / them.
Do you like	shopping for clothes?	I don't really like it / them.
		I don't like it / them (at all).
		I can't stand it / them.
		I hate it / them.
		It's / They're great!
		It's / They're OK.
		It's / They're not bad.
		I'm not sure. I've never tried / been to / gone…

PRACTICE 1

Class CD 1
Track 49

Listen to the example. Choose a big city that you know. Ask your partner about the following things. Add one more of your own and ask about it, too.

Student A asks about
1. small family-owned stores
2. fast-food restaurants
3. Thai food
4. traveling by bus
5. museums
6. your idea _____

Student B asks about
1. big department stores
2. expensive restaurants
3. Indian food
4. traveling by train
5. art galleries
6. your idea _____

Use These Words

It's / They're…   great.
fantastic.
exciting.
noisy.
expensive.
dangerous.
boring.

PRACTICE 2

Look at the list of things below. Mark your own likes or dislikes with a check (✓). Ask two other people about their likes and dislikes. Write their initials on the chart.

..............?	love	like	OK	don't really like	hate/ can't stand
Big cities					
Planes					
Video cameras					
Bus tours					
Museums					
Shopping for clothes					
Speaking English					

PRACTICE 3

Class CD 1 Track 50

Listen to the example. Then find a new partner and ask questions about the people he or she spoke with.

A: Does Masato like big cities?
B: Yes, he really likes them. / (No, he can't stand them.)
A: What about planes?
B: He thinks they're OK.

LISTEN TO THIS

Class CD 1 Track 51

Part 1 Listen to Alissa and Lee talk about their plans for tonight. What topics do they talk about?

Part 2 Listen again and check (✓) their opinions about each of the topics.

	Topic	Alissa		Lee	
		Likes	Dislikes	Likes	Dislikes
1					
2					
3					
4					
5					

Part 3 Talk to your partner about Alissa and Lee. What do they like or dislike?

LET'S TALK

Part 1 Check (✓) the things you like, and mark everything you dislike with an **✗**.

- ☐ swimming
- ☐ tennis
- ☐ dancing
- ☐ watching TV
- ☐ comic books
- ☐ going to clubs
- ☐ driving
- ☐ drinking coffee
- ☐ window shopping
- ☐ doing housework
- ☐ chatting on-line
- ☐ sleeping

- ☐ golf
- ☐ baseball
- ☐ singing karaoke
- ☐ video games
- ☐ movies
- ☐ cooking
- ☐ eating in restaurants
- ☐ shopping for clothes
- ☐ talking on the phone
- ☐ doing homework
- ☐ listening to music

Part 2 Try to find a person who likes at least three of the same things as you by asking questions.

A: Do you like swimming?
B: I love it! What do you think of golf?
A: I can't stand it!

Part 3 When you find a person who likes three of the same things as you, fill in the schedule below with a plan for your perfect day together.

When	What
Morning	
Afternoon	
Evening	

Conversation 2
I love sight-seeing!

What do you like to do in cities? What would you show a guest who is visiting your city?

Class CD 1, Track 52

Mike: This bus tour looks great! We can see the city in one day. I love bus tours!

Amy: Really? I can't stand bus tours! There's too much traffic for them.

Mike: Well, you told me the shopping here is really good. What do you think of going shopping for shoes?

Amy: Yes, you can get some real bargains. But I don't like those big shopping centers.

Mike: Neither do I!

Amy: How about going to the bird park? I love nature parks.

Mike: Yeah, so do I…um, but we only have one day! So let's go to the museum. We'll get a chance to see art that is never in the U.S.!

Amy: Good idea! And maybe there's a bus tour in the evening when there's not as much traffic. I know you love sight-seeing!

Mike: Let's check it out!

Student CD, Track 11

Class CD 1, Track 53
Pronunciation Focus

Listen and practice these words.

[s]	[sh]
city	shopping
sight	shoes
see	

Listen to the conversation again and notice how these words are pronounced.

GIVE IT A TRY

1. Agreeing and disagreeing with likes and dislikes

	Agree	Disagree	
I love it / them. I like it / them. I hate it / them.	Really? So do I. Me, too.	You do? Really?	I don't. I hate it / them.
I don't like it / them.	Neither do I. Me, neither.	You don't? Really?	I do. I like it / them.
I can't stand it / them.	Neither can I. Me, neither.	You can't? Really?	I like it / them.

PRACTICE 1

Class CD 1
Track 54

Listen to the example. Then decide with your partner whether the people below agree or disagree. Role-play their conversations. Reverse roles.

(1) I hate animated movies.

(2) I hate Italian food.

(3) I love cooking.

(4) I love golf.

PRACTICE 2

Write two things you like, two things you don't like, and two things you can't stand. Tell your partner. Does your partner agree or disagree? Check (✓) the box.

You	Your partner	
I like….	Agree	Disagree
1. _____	☐	☐
2. _____	☐	☐
I don't like….		
1. _____	☐	☐
2. _____	☐	☐
I can't stand….		
1. _____	☐	☐
2. _____	☐	☐

2. Stating preferences

> I like shopping, but I don't like eating out.
> He loves video games, but he can't stand shopping.

PRACTICE 1

Look at the lists below. Add three more choices in each category.

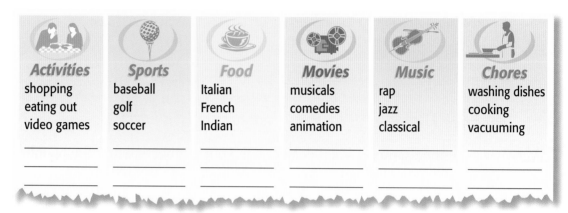

Activities	**Sports**	**Food**	**Movies**	**Music**	**Chores**
shopping	baseball	Italian	musicals	rap	washing dishes
eating out	golf	French	comedies	jazz	cooking
video games	soccer	Indian	animation	classical	vacuuming
_____	_____	_____	_____	_____	_____
_____	_____	_____	_____	_____	_____
_____	_____	_____	_____	_____	_____

PRACTICE 2

Class CD 1 Track 55

Listen to the example. Then work in groups. Choose a category and talk about something that you like and don't like. Take turns until everybody has had a turn.

A: I like shopping, but I don't like eating out.
B: I love video games, but I hate shopping.
C: I love shopping too, but I can't stand video games.

LISTEN TO THIS

Class CD 1 Track 56

Part 1 Listen to the conversations and write the topics you hear.

Part 2 Listen again and decide if the speakers agree or disagree. Check (✓) the correct answer.

	Topic	Agree	Disagree
1.			
2.			
3.			
4.			

Part 3 Listen again for each of the following expressions. Do they show agreement or disagreement? Write *A* or *D* next to each one.

1. To be honest… ____
2. Sounds perfect! ____
3. Really? ____
4. I know what you mean. ____

(Student A looks at this page. Student B looks at page 110.)

Part 1 You are Katya. Here are your likes and dislikes. Your partner is Joe. Find out which likes and dislikes you share and write them in the chart below.

My likes	My dislikes	Joe's likes	Joe's dislikes
swimming and scuba diving	sunbathing and lying on the beach		
sight-seeing and museums	loud music and dancing		
eating exotic food	shopping		

Part 2 Choose which of these three vacations would be ideal for you and your partner.

ISTANBUL

A HISTORY LOVER'S PARADISE— Greek and Roman ruins, palaces and castles of the Ottoman emperors.

SPEND A DAY IN THE BAZAAR— shopping for silk rugs, silver jewelry, or leather jackets.

EAT IN A TRADITIONAL TURKISH RESTAURANT— have stuffed eggplant, dumplings with yogurt, and famous Turkish pastries for dessert.

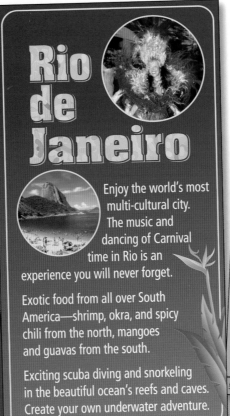

Rio de Janeiro

Enjoy the world's most multi-cultural city. The music and dancing of Carnival time in Rio is an experience you will never forget.

Exotic food from all over South America—shrimp, okra, and spicy chili from the north, mangoes and guavas from the south.

Exciting scuba diving and snorkeling in the beautiful ocean's reefs and caves. Create your own underwater adventure.

CHIANG MAI

Enjoy the beautiful animals and natural scenery of the jungle, trekking and climbing in the nearby hills.

Visit ancient temples, and learn about yoga and meditation.

Unique handmade goods—choose from hand-woven cloth, paintings, statues, and silver jewelry.

Now Try This

Make a list of things you plan to do on your three-day vacation. Plan your schedule for each day.

Conversation 1
How about coming with us?

How often do you go out? Where? Do you usually go out with one friend or a group?

CONSIDER THIS

The world's most expensive dinner?

The Eagle Club in Gstaad, Switzerland, serves club members only, and membership costs about €40,000. And you may have to wait: it takes about three years to approve new members.

- What's the most expensive meal you have ever eaten?
- What's the most delicious meal you have ever eaten?

Class CD 1, Track 57

Debby: Hi, Masato.

Masato: Hi, Debby. How's it going?

Debby: I'm OK. How are you doing?

Masato: Pretty good. Listen, have you heard about the new Thai restaurant over on University Avenue?

Debby: Do you mean The Bangkok?

Masato: That's the one. A bunch of us are going over there for dinner tomorrow night. How about coming with us?

Debby: Sure. I'd love to.

Masato: Great. I'll call and make a reservation.

Debby: Any time after 6:00 is good for me. Oh! I'm late! I have to go to class.

Masato: All right. I'll call you tonight and tell you the time.

Debby: Great. Talk to you then.

Student CD, Track 12

1. Accepting invitations

Do you feel like What about How about	going out for dinner	Saturday? tonight?	Sure. OK.	I'd love to. That's a good idea. Why not?

PRACTICE

Class CD 1
Track 58

Listen to the example. Then invite your partner to do the following things.
Reverse roles.

1. going out for dinner next Friday
2. seeing a movie Sunday afternoon
3. going for coffee tomorrow after class

4. playing tennis Saturday morning
5. going camping this weekend
6. your idea _____

2. Declining invitations

Do you want to Would you like to	have lunch tomorrow?	
Oh, I'm sorry, I can't.	I have to I've got to	study.
That's too bad. Maybe next time.		

Use These Words

go swimming	go out for lunch
go shopping	go for coffee
go dancing	go for a drive
go out for dinner	go for a walk

PRACTICE

Class CD 1
Track 59

Listen to the example. Then invite your partner to do the following things. He or
she is busy and makes an excuse. Reverse roles. Add your own idea to each list.

Invitations

1. go to a party tonight
2. see a movie Friday night
3. go bowling on Sunday
4. go shopping on Saturday
5. your idea _____

Excuses

1. work late
2. meet a friend
3. visit my parents
4. take a test
5. your idea _____

Unit 6 **45**

3. Getting more information

Would you like to Do you want to	come to a party this Saturday?
Sounds good.	Where is it? Who's going?
It's at my place / Dave's. Some people from work / school.	

Class CD 1
Track 60
Listen to the example. Then invite your partner to the following events. Your partner will ask for extra information. Reverse roles. Fill in the blanks with your own ideas and information.

Event	Extra information
1. come to a party	Where is it? What time does it start? Who's going?
2. go to a baseball game	Who's playing? Where is it? How much are the tickets?
3. go out for dinner	Where are you going? What kind of food do they have?
4. go for a drive	Where are you going? How long will the drive be?
5. see a movie	
6. go swimming	
7. your idea:	

LISTEN TO THIS

Class CD 1
Track 61

Part 1 Listen to two conversations. What are the people in the conversations going to do?

Part 2 Listen again and fill in the missing information.

	What	**Where**	**When**	**Extra information**
Misa / Yvette				
Oscar / Ben				

Part 3 Describe what Misa and Yvette are going to do. Describe what Oscar and Ben are going to do.

LET'S TALK

Part 1 This is your date book for next week. Choose five things from the list and write them in your date book.

Daily Planner

MORNING   AFTERNOON   EVENING

| Sunday | Monday | Tuesday | | Wednesday | Thursday | Friday | Saturday |

have coffee
see a baseball game
go to a disco
go out for lunch

go out for dinner
go swimming
go to a karaoke club
go shopping

go to a movie
go to a rock concert
go skateboarding
go dancing

Part 2 Invite your classmates to join you for the five activities. You can invite as many classmates as you like but you can only do one activity with each classmate. Remember to ask for additional information. Try to fill up your date book.

Part 3 When your date book is full, tell your partner about your plans for next week.

Conversation 2
Why don't we meet there?

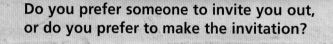

Do you prefer someone to invite you out, or do you prefer to make the invitation?

Class CD 1, Track 62

Masato: Hello?

Karen: Hello. Could I speak to Masato, please?

Masato: Speaking.

Karen: Oh, hi, Masato. This is Karen Harris. We met at Chris and Jim's party.

Masato: Of course. How're you?

Karen: Great. Uh, Masato, would you like to see the Rocket Dogs on Thursday night? They're at the Garage Club.

Masato: Oh, I'm sorry, Karen, but I can't. I have to work late this Thursday.

Karen: Oh…that's too bad.

Masato: Yeah. I really like the Rocket Dogs.

Karen: Actually, are you doing anything on Friday or Saturday? They're playing those two nights as well.

Masato: Well, I can't make it on Friday either, but I'm free on Saturday night. What time does it start?

Karen: At eight sharp. How about meeting in front of the club at about a quarter after seven?

Masato: That sounds perfect. And let's go out for coffee after the show.

Karen: Sure!

Masato: OK, see you at 7:15, Saturday.

Student CD, Track 13

Class CD 1, Track 63
Pronunciation Focus

Listen to the questions in the conversation. Does the intonation rise or fall?

Could I speak to Masato, please?

How're you?

What time does it start?

Listen to the conversation again and mark the intonation of each question.

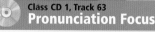

GIVE IT A TRY

1. Suggesting another day

> A: I'm really sorry. I can't make it.

> B: OK. Maybe we can do it some other time then.
> A: Yes, I'd really like to.

> B: Oh, that's too bad. Well, how about Friday, then?
> A: Great! That sounds good.

PRACTICE

Class CD 1 Track 64
Listen to the example. Then invite your partner to do something. He or she is busy and can't accept. Suggest another time or day. Reverse roles.

2. Setting the time and the place

Where do you want to meet?	How about meeting in front of the club? Why don't we meet at the restaurant? Let's meet at the coffee shop.
Great. What time?	Why don't we meet at 7:15? How about 7:15? Let's meet at 7:15.
Fine. See you at 7:15 / then.	OK. See you!

PRACTICE

Class CD 1 Track 65
Listen to the example. Then invite your partner to do something. He or she accepts. Set the time and place. Reverse roles.

① LIVE Rocket Dogs Saturday 7:30 Garage Club

② Sunday 2:00 Olympia Stadium SKATEBOARDING SUPERSTARS

③ Numero Uno Bistro 7-11:30 Live Music from 8:30

④ Technorock Dance Club 10-3a.m. Music by DJ Technoray

3. Changing plans

| Could we meet | outside the station instead? at 7:00? a little later / earlier? | Sure. No problem. |

PRACTICE

Class CD 1
Track 66
Listen to the example. Then invite your partner to do something and arrange a time and a place to meet. Your partner will suggest a different place and time. Reverse roles.

4. Adding to plans

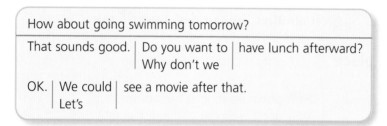

How about going swimming tomorrow?		
That sounds good.	Do you want to Why don't we	have lunch afterward?
OK.	We could Let's	see a movie after that.

PRACTICE

Class CD 1
Track 67
Listen to the example. Student A invites Student B to do two of the following activities. Student B adds an activity to the plan. Reverse roles.

Student A's invitations
1. go swimming
2. play soccer
3. meet downtown for lunch
4. come over and watch videos

Student B's suggestions
1. have lunch first
2. watch TV
3. do some shopping afterward
4. order a pizza for dinner

LISTEN TO THIS

Class CD 1
Track 68
Part 1 Listen to a conversation between Sandy and Lisa. Student A will write down all the different times. Student B will write down all the types of restaurants. Student C will write down all the types of sports.

Student A	Student B	Student C

Part 2 Listen again. Write down Sandy and Lisa's schedule in the correct order.

1	2	3

Part 3 Talk about what Sandy and Lisa are going to do this evening.

(Student A looks at this page. Student B looks at page 111.)

Part 1 Your friend is going to visit your town this weekend. Talk with him or her on the phone and plan your daily schedule. Try to do as many things as you can. Talk about the time and day you will go to each place or event. Your friend will arrive at 7:00 P.M. on Friday night and leave at 4:00 P.M. on Sunday.

You also found the following information in your local newspaper.

This Weekend

Viva Latina
Mexican restaurant
Lunch 12–3,
Dinner 5–midnight

Baseball Game
The Red Rovers v. the Supergiants,
Saturday 3:00 p.m.

Gold Star Movie House
French Film Festival,
Sad December
Sat–Sun, 3:00, 5:30

Karaoke Club
Open all day,
Food from 7:00 p.m.
to 11:30 p.m.

...cert
...al,
...ber
...0, 5:30

Chagall art exhibition
Museum of Modern Art,
Tue–Sun 9:00 a.m.
to 5:00 p.m.
until 8 p.m. on Fridays

Videocafe
Newest music videos and video games,
10–midnight

Rock concert
Techno Live Dance Club,
8 until late

Friday 7:00 P.M.
Meet at train station

Part 2 When you have planned your weekend, discuss your schedule with another pair of students. How are they different?

Now Try This

Imagine that you have a change of plan. You have to visit your grandmother on Saturday afternoon. Call your friend and rearrange your schedule.

Review:
Units 4–6

LISTEN TO THIS UNIT 4

Class CD 1 Track 69 *Part 1* Listen to the message about movies today. Write the missing information.

	Start time	End time	Extra information
Galactica			
Mask of the Mummy			
Broken Window			

Part 2 Ask your partner questions to find out if your answers are the same.

GIVE IT A TRY

Write the places on the map. Don't show your partner. Now ask your partner where his or her places are. Mark them on your map. Then compare maps.

1. pharmacy
2. dry cleaner's
3. restaurant
4. bookstore
5. library
6. gift store
7. post office
8. supermarket

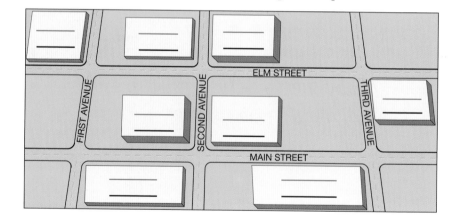

LISTEN TO THIS UNIT 5

Class CD 1 Track 70 *Part 1* Listen to the conversation between Mike and Bernie. Check (✔) the things they like and mark the things they dislike with an ✗. Do Mike and Bernie agree or disagree?

	Mike	Bernie	Agree / Disagree
Getting up early			
Jogging			
Swimming			
Staying up late			

Part 2 Ask your partner questions to find out if your answers are the same.

GIVE IT A TRY

On a piece of paper, write one thing that you like, dislike, or can't stand. Walk around the room and find out how many people like or dislike your topic. Make notes of the reasons for people's opinions. Finally, give a report to the class on the results of your survey.

Your topic: _____

Student name	Like, Dislike, Can't stand	Reason

LISTEN TO THIS UNIT 6

Class CD 1
Track 71

Part 1 Listen to Carla and Maria talking about their plans for the weekend. First write the different events they talk about. Then add as many extra details as you can.

	What?	Where?	When?	Extra information
1				
2				
3				

Part 2 Ask your partner questions to find out if your answers are the same.

GIVE IT A TRY

Work in groups. Students A and B: You are visiting your town for one day. Students C and D: You want to show your visitors the best things in your town, go out for lunch, and go out in the evening. Make a list of things to do and decide on your schedule for the day.

Monday, March 5

9:00 a.m. _____

10:00 a.m. _____

11:00 a.m. _____

12:00 p.m. _____

1:00 p.m. _____

2:00 p.m. _____

3:00 p.m. _____

4:00 p.m. _____

5:00 p.m. _____

6:00 p.m. _____

7:00 p.m. _____

8:00 p.m. _____

9:00 p.m. _____

March
S M T W T F S
            1 2 3
4 5 6 7 8 9 10
11 12 13 14 15 16 17
18 19 20 21 22 23 24
25 26 27 28 29 30 31

Conversation 1
Could you help me?

Which clothes in the picture would you buy?

CONSIDER THIS

Online shopping

People love shopping on the Internet. They like the convenience and low prices on-line. But they worry about giving their credit card number and about not receiving their order.

- Do you shop on the Internet? Why or why not?
- If you do, what do you buy?
- Do you know anyone who buys on-line?

Hot products on-lir

- books   ● music
- videos   ● clothir
- computer items

Class CD 2, Track 2

Salesperson:	Can I help you?
Naoko:	Yes, please. We're looking for men's shirts.
Salesperson:	They're right over there by the escalator.
Kohei:	Here we are.
Naoko:	Look at this one! The color is perfect for you!
Kohei:	Hmm…I like it, too. How much is it?
Naoko:	It's on sale for $19.98.
Kohei:	That's a good price, but I think they only have it in large.
Naoko:	Well, why don't we ask someone? Excuse me. Could you help us?
Salesperson:	Sure, what can I do for you?
Kohei:	Does this shirt come in medium?
Salesperson:	Yes, it does. Let's see…. Here's a medium.
Kohei:	Great. I'll take it.
Salesperson:	Will that be cash or credit?

Student CD, Track 14

GIVE IT A TRY

1. Getting and giving help

Excuse me.	Could	you help me?	Sure. How can I help you?
	Can		Certainly. What can I help you with?
			do for you?

Can I help you?	No, thanks. I'm just looking.
Is there something I can help you with?	Yes, please. I'm looking for men's shirts.

PRACTICE 1

Class CD 2 Track 3 Listen to the example. You are in a department store. Your partner is a salesperson. Ask him or her for help. Reverse roles.

PRACTICE 2

Class CD 2 Track 4 Listen to the example. You are a salesperson in a department store. Your partner is a customer. Ask if he or she needs help. Reverse roles.

2. Getting information

Do you have	this (sweater) in black?	Yes, we do.
	these in size 10?	No, I'm sorry. We don't.
	any other colors?	We can order one for you.
Does this come	in black?	Yes, it does.
Do these come	in medium?	Yes, they do.
	in size 8?	No, I'm sorry It doesn't.
	in a larger / smaller size?	They don't.

PRACTICE

Class CD 2 Track 5 Listen to the example. Then imagine your partner is a salesperson. Ask for information about two of the items in the ads below. Reverse roles.

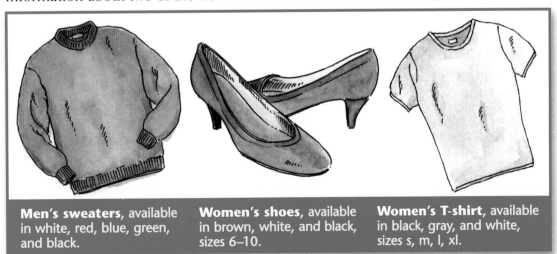

Men's sweaters, available in white, red, blue, green, and black.

Women's shoes, available in brown, white, and black, sizes 6–10.

Women's T-shirt, available in black, gray, and white, sizes s, m, l, xl.

3. Asking prices

Excuse me. How much	is	this jacket? it?	(It's)	$249.
	are	these shoes? they?	(They're)	$74.99.
Is it / Are they on sale? Is there a discount?			Yes, it's Yes, they're	$10.00 off. reduced to $99. half price.
Great. I'll take it / them. No, thanks. It's / They're too expensive.			Will that be cash or credit? OK. Can I help you with anything else?	

Class CD 2
Track 6

Use These Words

sweater	shirt	T-shirt
dress	coat	jacket

a pair of:
pants	shoes	socks
jeans	shorts	

PRACTICE

Listen to the example. Then ask your partner the price of the following items. Reverse roles.

Student A asks about

1. shoes
2. T-shirt
3. coat

Student B gives information about

1. shoes ($74.99)
2. T-shirts ($10.00 each, or 3 for $25.00)
3. coat ($199 reduced to $99.00)

Student A gives information about

1. silk scarf ($150, now half price)
2. dress ($269)
3. jeans ($40.00, now $10.00 off)

Student B asks about

1. silk scarf
2. dress
3. jeans

LISTEN TO THIS

Class CD 2
Track 7

Part 1 Listen to conversations between Sumiko, Yoshi, and three salespeople in a department store. What three items do they want to buy?

Part 2 Listen again and write the information from the assistant.

	Item 1	Item 2	Item 3
Sizes available			
Colors available			
Price			

Part 3 What do Sumiko and Yoshi buy? Describe each item and why they bought it (or didn't buy it).

Part 1 Make up prices and write them down next to each clothing item below. You are going to sell these items to your classmates. You can have discounts and provide different sizes.

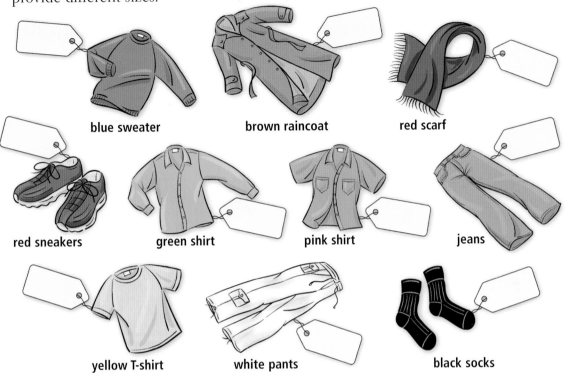

blue sweater   brown raincoat   red scarf

red sneakers   green shirt   pink shirt   jeans

yellow T-shirt   white pants   black socks

Part 2 You have $250 to spend on clothes. With this amount of money, buy as many items as you can from your classmates. At the same time, try to sell all the items in your list in Part 1 to others. Don't show your page to your partner.

RULES

You can buy only one item from each classmate.

When you buy an item, write it in the list below, with the price and name of the person you bought it from. Remember to ask about different sizes and colors, as well as discounts.

When you sell an item, put a ✔ next to the picture above.

When you have sold all your clothing items and spent all your money, sit down with a partner.

Item/Price/Name of person: **Item/Price/Name of person:**

1. _____   4. _____

2. _____   5. _____

3. _____   6. _____

Part 3 Tell your partner about the items you bought. What sizes and colors did you get? Did you get any discounts? Do you have any money left over? Reverse roles.

Conversation 2
This sweater is more stylish.

Do you sometimes return things to a store? Why?

Class CD 2, Track 8

Naoko:	Excuse me. Could you help me? I'd like to exchange this sweater.
Salesperson:	What's the problem with it?
Naoko:	My boyfriend bought this for me, but I don't like it. It's too old-fashioned. I want something more stylish.
Salesperson:	I see…well, why don't you look around?
Miriam:	These two sweaters are nice. Why don't you try them on?
Naoko:	OK, which one do you like better?
Miriam:	This gray sweater is cute! This kind of collar is very fashionable now.
Naoko:	Really? I kind of like the black one. It's longer and looser, so I think it'll be more comfortable.
Miriam:	Yes, but the gray one really suits you. It's more stylish than the black one.
Salesperson:	The gray one is a better quality and it's the same price as the one you're exchanging.
Naoko:	You've talked me into it! I'll take this one instead.
Salesperson:	No problem. I'll switch them for you.

Student CD, Track 15

Class CD 2, Track 9
Pronunciation Focus

In American English, *t* in the middle of a word is pronounced /d/. Listen and practice these words.

sweater	it'll
better	quality

Listen to the conversation again and notice the /d/ sounds in the middle of words. Can you think of any more examples?

GIVE IT A TRY

1. Comparing things (1)

Which	hat	do you like better?
	boots	

I like	the gray hat	better than	the blue one.
	this hat		that one.
	the red boots		the white ones.
	these boots		those (ones).

PRACTICE

Class CD 2 Track 10

Listen to the example. Then ask your partner which one(s) he or she prefers. Reverse roles.

gray hat / blue hat   high boots / low boots
tight sweater / loose sweater   wide jeans / narrow jeans
cotton shirt / polyester shirt   thin belt / wide belt

2. Comparing things (2)

Why do you like	the gray hat	better?
	the brown boots	

I like it / them because it's / they're more stylish than the black one(s).

PRACTICE

Class CD 2 Track 11

Listen to the example. Then look at the pictures. Ask your partner which one of the items he or she prefers, and then ask why. Reverse roles.

Use These Words

wider / narrower
longer / shorter
thinner / thicker
tighter / looser
more stylish / more old-fashioned
more expensive / cheaper
plainer / fancier

3. Returning things

I'd like to	exchange	this sweater.	What's the problem with it / them?
	return	these shoes.	What's wrong with it / them?
It's too old-fashioned. It doesn't fit. They don't work. I don't really like them.			Of course, we can	exchange it / them. give you a refund. Do you have your receipt? I'm sorry. We don't give refunds. I'll speak to the manager.

PRACTICE

Class CD 2
Track 12

Listen to the example. Your partner is a salesperson. Choose two of the items below and ask for a refund or an exchange. Reverse roles.

LISTEN TO THIS

Class CD 2
Track 13

Part 1 Listen to three customers who want to return items to a department store. What items do they want to return? Write them in the chart.

Part 2 Listen again and write the reasons why they want to return these items and the result.

	Item	Reason	Result
1			
2			
3			

Part 3 Which customer had the best reason for a refund?

(Student A looks at this page. Student B looks at page 112.)

Part 1 You are planning a trip to Canada this winter and you need to buy pants, a jacket, and socks. Your favorite color is purple. Your clothing size is large. Your shoe size is 8. Read the information from Sam's clothing catalog and decide which items you want to buy.

Part 2 Write down the items you will buy. Call the clothing catalog company and order the items you need. How much did you spend?

Sam's Outdoor Clothing

Pure wool or cotton / polyester pants, wide or narrow styles	Four-season nylon / down mix ski jackets, long or short styles	Hiking socks, 100% wool or cotton
Colors: _____	**Colors:** _____	**Colors:** _____
Sizes: _____	**Sizes:** _____	**Sizes:** _____
Price: _____	**Price:** _____	**Price:** _____
Your order: _____	**Your order:** _____	**Your order:** _____

Part 3 You are a sales representative for Eddy's clothing catalog company. A customer will call you with his or her order. Explain which items are on sale or not available. Persuade the customer to buy as many items as possible. Write down the customer's order.

EDDY'S OUTDOOR CLOTHING

Genuine leather or nylon backpacks, waterproof, lightweight	Leather hiking sandals, high- or low-heel styles	Comfortable round-neck T-shirts, 100% cotton
Colors: black, purple	**Colors:** black, blue, brown	**Colors:** yellow, purple, red
Sizes: one size	**Sizes:** sizes 6-10	**Sizes:** s, m, l
Price: leather $89 or nylon $69 (nylon backpack on sale this week for $49)	**Price:** $70 (half price this week only)	**Price:** $6.50 each (three for $15.00)
Customer's order: _____	**Customer's order:** _____	**Customer's order:** _____

Now Try This

One of the items you bought in Part 2 has a problem. Call the company, explain what is wrong, and ask for a refund or an exchange.

Conversation 1
And what would you like?

What do you usually eat for breakfast?

CONSIDER THIS

Durian is a fruit that's popular in Southeast Asia. People say it tastes like onion ice cream! Rattlesnake is snake meat that's served in the southwestern U.S. People say it tastes like chicken!

● Have you eaten either of these foods? Would you like to?

Class CD 2, Track 14

Jason: Everything looks good. What are you going to have, Akemi?

Akemi: I think I'll have pancakes and a cup of tea. How about you? What are you having?

Jason: Pancakes sound good, but I feel like having scrambled eggs. I guess we're ready to order. Excuse me!

Server: Good morning. Have you decided yet?

Akemi: Yes, I'll have pancakes and a cup of tea.

Server: What kind of pancakes would you like? We have blueberry, apple, or buttermilk.

Akemi: Apple, please.

Server: What kind of juice would you like?

Akemi: Tomato juice, please.

Server: OK. And what would you like, sir?

Jason: I'd like scrambled eggs. With apple juice, please.

Server: Would you like bacon or toast with that?

Jason: Toast, please.

Server: Any tea or coffee?

Jason: Coffee for me.

Server: Thank you. I'll be right back with your drinks.

Akemi: Thank you.

GIVE IT A TRY

1. Discussing the menu

| What are you | going to have, | Akemi? |
| | having, | |

(I think) I'll have pancakes and a cup of tea.

PRACTICE

Class CD 2 Track 15

Listen to the example. You're at a restaurant having breakfast with a friend. Ask what he or she wants to eat and drink. Answer using the menu below. Reverse roles.

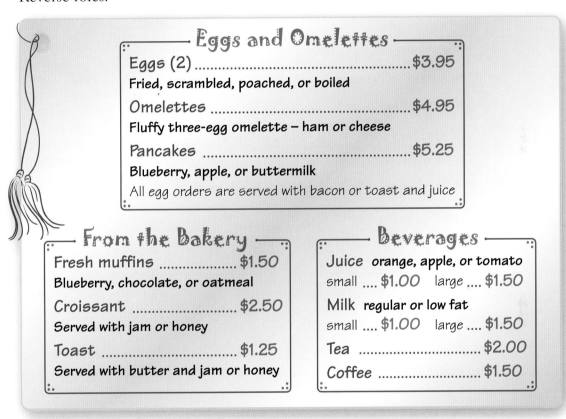

Eggs and Omelettes

Eggs (2) $3.95
Fried, scrambled, poached, or boiled

Omelettes $4.95
Fluffy three-egg omelette – ham or cheese

Pancakes $5.25
Blueberry, apple, or buttermilk

All egg orders are served with bacon or toast and juice

From the Bakery

Fresh muffins $1.50
Blueberry, chocolate, or oatmeal

Croissant $2.50
Served with jam or honey

Toast $1.25
Served with butter and jam or honey

Beverages

Juice orange, apple, or tomato
small .... $1.00   large $1.50

Milk regular or low fat
small .... $1.00   large $1.50

Tea $2.00

Coffee $1.50

2. Ordering

What	would you like?	I think I'll have	scrambled eggs. With toast, please.
	will you have?		coffee. No cream, please.
Are you ready to order?		I'm not sure yet. I'm still trying to decide.
Have you decided yet?		Could we have a few more minutes, please?

PRACTICE

Class CD 2 Track 16

Listen to the example. Then choose something from the menu and your partner will take your order. Reverse roles.

3. Adding extra information to your order

Would you like toast or bacon?
(I'd like) | toast, please.
(I'll have) |

What kind of juice would you like?
(I'd like) | tomato juice, please.
(I'll have) |

Menu

Today's Lunch Specials

Chicken Fingers

Crab and Asparagus Quiche

Hot Roast Beef Sandwich

Salmon Teriyaki

All specials come with your choice of:

Cream of Mushroom Soup or Green Salad (French or Oil & Vinegar dressing)

Potatoes: Baked, Mashed, or French Fries

Vegetables: Carrots, Spinach, or Green Beans

Dessert: Vanilla Ice Cream or Fresh Fruit

PRACTICE

Class CD 2 Track 17

Listen to the example. Student A is the customer. Student B is the server and will ask the customer about three of the following items. Reverse roles.

1. soup or salad   2. salad dressing   3. potatoes   4. vegetables   5. dessert

A: Excuse me.

B: Good afternoon. What would you like?

A: I'd like the hot roast beef sandwich.

B: Yes, sir. Would you like soup or salad with that?

A: I'd like a salad, please.

B: What kind of dressing would you like?

A: French, please.

B: And what kind of dessert would you like?

A: Vanilla ice cream, please.

Part 1 Listen to a group of friends having dinner together at Tammy's Diner. Write down the names of all the foods you hear.

Part 2 Listen again and write the food next to the correct name.

Wen	
Dave	
Anne	
Lisa	

Part 3 What is the combined order for the whole group?

LET'S TALK

Part 1 Read the lunch menu. Circle the food you want. Choose one item from each section. Don't forget to circle all the additional information, too.

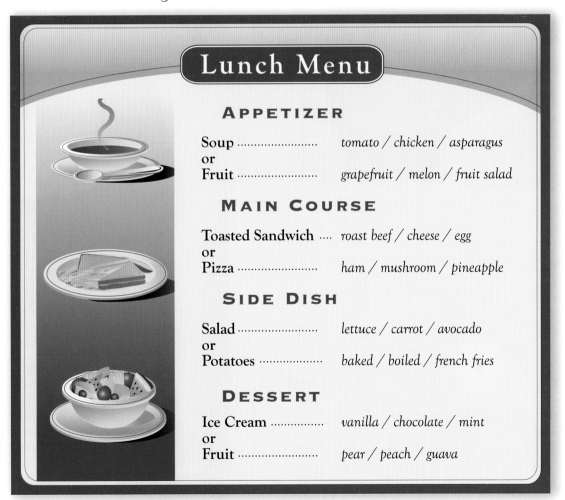

Lunch Menu

APPETIZER

Soup .... tomato / chicken / asparagus
or
Fruit .... grapefruit / melon / fruit salad

MAIN COURSE

Toasted Sandwich .... roast beef / cheese / egg
or
Pizza .... ham / mushroom / pineapple

SIDE DISH

Salad .... lettuce / carrot / avocado
or
Potatoes .... baked / boiled / french fries

DESSERT

Ice Cream .... vanilla / chocolate / mint
or
Fruit .... pear / peach / guava

Part 2 Don't show your menu to anyone. Ask your classmates questions to find someone who has made the same choices as you.

Conversation 2
Would you care for any dessert?

Do you like to try new foods? What is the most unusual food you have ever eaten?

Class CD 2, Track 19

Server: OK, so that's two chicken burritos and one order of nacho chips with spicy salsa.

Akemi: Could you tell me what gazpacho is, please?

Server: Sure, it's a spicy soup served cold. It's made from tomatoes and vegetables.

Eun-mi: Hmm…That sounds good. I'll have one of those, please.

Server: Would you like something to drink with that?

Akemi: Do you have any iced tea?

Server: I'm sorry, we don't. We have lemonade or soda.

Akemi: I'll have lemonade, then.

Eun-mi: Make it two.

Server: Would you like to order a dessert now?

Eun-mi: No, thank you. We'll wait until later.

Akemi: You know, they have fantastic flan here.

Eun-mi: They do? Well, maybe we could split one. We'll have one flan, please.

Server: Would you like me to bring two spoons?

Akemi: Yes, please. That's a good idea.

Student CD, Track 17

Class CD 2, Track 20
Pronunciation Focus

Would and *you* are often linked together in spoken English to sound like *wouldya*.

Would you like something to drink?

Would you like to order a dessert now?

Would you like me to bring two spoons?

Listen to the conversation again and notice the linked words.

GIVE IT A TRY

1. Describing food

> Could you tell me what gazpacho is?
> What's gazpacho made from?
> Could you tell me what's in gazpacho?
>
> It's | a spicy soup served cold.
> | made from tomatoes and vegetables.

PRACTICE

Class CD 2 Track 21

Listen to the example. Then ask your partner about three of these foods. Reverse roles. Fill in the blanks with your own ideas.

1. gazpacho / a spicy soup served cold / made from tomatoes and vegetables
2. burrito / a soft pancake / filled with meat or vegetables
3. corn chowder / creamy soup / made from corn and potato
4. sushi / cooked rice with pieces of raw fish
5. takoyaki / small balls / made from octopus and flour
6. kimchi / pickled cabbage / spicy
7. your idea _____
8. your idea _____

Use These Words

fried	spicy
steamed	salty
boiled	sweet
baked	creamy
grilled	crunchy
pickled	smooth

2. Offering additional food or drink

| Would you like | something | to drink? | Do you have any iced tea? |
Would you care for	anything		
Yes, certainly.			One iced tea, please.
I'm sorry, we don't. We have lemonade or soda.			I'll have lemonade, then.
I'm afraid we've run out.			

PRACTICE

Class CD 2 Track 22

Listen to the example. Student A is the server. Student B is the customer. Student B will ask for three of the following drinks. If they are not available, choose something else. Reverse roles.

1. iced tea
2. lemonade
3. hot chocolate
4. ginger ale
5. cappuccino

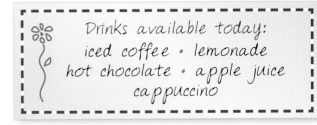

Drinks available today:
iced coffee · lemonade
hot chocolate · apple juice
cappuccino

3. Offering other suggestions

Would you like	anything else?	Yes, could you bring me	some more rolls?
Would you care for	some dessert?		some flan?
	some more coffee?	No, thank you.	
Would you like me to bring you the check?		Not right now, thank you.	
		Just the bill / check, please.	

PRACTICE

Class CD 2
Track 23

Listen to the example. Then ask your partner about three of the following. Your partner will reply with a request. Reverse roles.

1. anything else? / some more rolls
2. dessert? / some flan
3. coffee? / a cappuccino
4. more tea? / some water
5. more rolls? / the check
6. your idea _____? / _____

LISTEN TO THIS

Class CD 2
Track 24

Part 1 Listen to three conversations. Write down what each person orders.

Part 2 Listen again and write down the choices available for each type of food or drink.

	Order	Choices available
1		
2		
3		

Part 3 What other choices could you add to each category?

(Student A looks at this page. Student B looks at page 113.)

Part 1 Read the menu. Put a check (✓) next to the dishes you want to order. Underline the dishes you need more information about.

Part 2 Go to the restaurant and order your meal. Ask questions about the items you don't understand.

Menu

Appetizer

Soup of the Day

Avocado Florentine

Dessert

Flan, Fresh Fruit Salad

Main Course

Roast Lamb and Vegetable Kebabs

Seafood Paella with Spicy Salsa

Beverages

Tea, Coffee, Herbal Tea

Part 3 Now you are the server. Answer the questions from the customer. Offer additional suggestions for desserts, drinks, or side dishes.

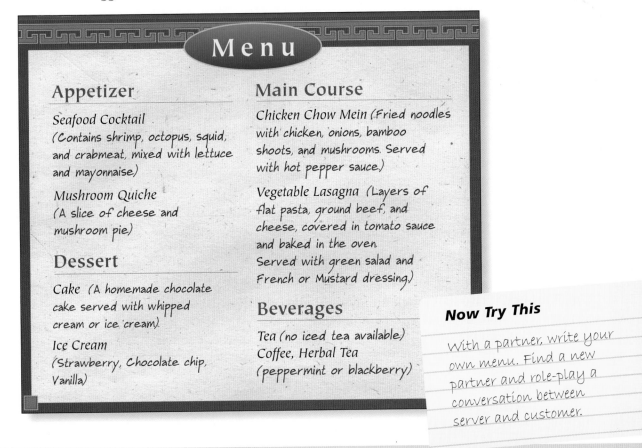

Menu

Appetizer

Seafood Cocktail
(Contains shrimp, octopus, squid, and crabmeat, mixed with lettuce and mayonnaise)

Mushroom Quiche
(A slice of cheese and mushroom pie)

Dessert

Cake (A homemade chocolate cake served with whipped cream or ice cream)

Ice Cream
(Strawberry, Chocolate chip, Vanilla)

Main Course

Chicken Chow Mein (Fried noodles with chicken, onions, bamboo shoots, and mushrooms. Served with hot pepper sauce.)

Vegetable Lasagna (Layers of flat pasta, ground beef, and cheese, covered in tomato sauce and baked in the oven.
Served with green salad and French or Mustard dressing.)

Beverages

Tea (no iced tea available)
Coffee, Herbal Tea
(peppermint or blackberry)

Now Try This

With a partner, write your own menu. Find a new partner and role-play a conversation between server and customer.

Unit 9

Conversation 1
Could I borrow that?

Do friends sometimes borrow things from you? Are there some things you don't like to lend?

CONSIDER THIS
1964 Winter Olympic Games

Italian bobsledder Eugenio Monti let Tony Nash of Great Britain borrow a part from the Italian bobsled to repair the British sled, which had broken. The British team won gold. Monti won the first International Fair Play Trophy.

● Have you ever let someone borrow something that helped them a lot?

Class CD 2, Track 25

Uma:	What's the matter, Sunya?
Sunya:	Can you believe this? I need to buy a birthday gift for my mother after class today, and I left my credit card at home.
Uma:	So what are you going to do?
Sunya:	I don't know…. Could you lend me some money?
Uma:	How much do you need?
Sunya:	Oh…about $30.00.
Uma:	I don't have that much on me right now.
Sunya:	Oh, well, do you think I could borrow your cell phone? I'll call my sister and ask her to get my credit card and meet me at the store.
Uma:	Sure. That's no problem. Just don't talk forever, OK?
Sunya:	Don't worry…thanks, I really appreciate it.

Student CD, Track 18

GIVE IT A TRY

1. Making small requests

| Excuse me. | Could I borrow a | pencil, please? |
| | Do you have an extra | piece of paper? |

Sure. Here you are / go.
I'm sorry. I don't have one / any.

PRACTICE 1

Class CD 2
Track 26

Listen to the example. Then ask for four of the following items. Your partner will accept or refuse. Your partner must give a reason. Reverse roles.

1. pencil
2. pen
3. dictionary
4. dime

5. piece of paper
6. ruler
7. quarter
8. eraser

PRACTICE 2

Think of four small things you want to borrow. Walk around the class and ask your classmates. When you have all four things, return to your seat.

2. Making larger requests

| Do you think I could borrow | $25 | until Tuesday? |
| Would you mind lending me | your laptop | for a few hours? |

| I'm sorry. | I don't have $25. |
| | I need it right now. |

But I left my wallet at home and I need to buy my school textbook.
But my computer isn't working and I have to write a report.

Can I let you know later?
OK. You can have it after I'm done.

PRACTICE

Class CD 2
Track 27

Listen to the example. Student A makes four requests. Student B refuses and gives a reason. Student A explains why he or she made the request. Reverse roles. Add your own ideas.

1. your car for the afternoon
2. $100 until next Friday
3. computer for the weekend
4. sleeping bag for the week
5. cell phone for the weekend
6. new motorcycle for an hour
7. CD player for a party on Saturday
8. your idea _____

Can I borrow $10.00?   I can lend you $10.00.

3. Asking for favors

Would you please Could you	open the door (for me)? turn on the lights? hold my coat?	Sure. No problem. Of course. I'd be glad to. I'm sorry. I can't (right now).

PRACTICE 1

Class CD 2
Track 28

Listen to the example. Then ask your partner to do three of these favors for you. Your partner accepts. Reverse roles. Add your own ideas.

1. open the window
2. turn up the volume
3. carry my bag

4. hold my books for a second
5. explain the homework
6. your idea _____

PRACTICE 2

Class CD 2
Track 29

Listen to the example. Then ask your partner to do three of the favors in Practice 1. This time, your partner refuses and gives a reason. Reverse roles. Add your own ideas.

> **Use These Words**
>
> My hands are full.
> I can't reach!
> I'm already carrying too much.
> It's too heavy.
> I'd like to, but I can't.
> I'm too busy.
> I'm in a hurry.

LISTEN TO THIS

Part 1 Look at the pictures. What kind of request is each picture about? Write the requests in your notebook.

Class CD 2
Track 30

Part 2 Listen to the conversations. Number the pictures in the correct order.

Part 3 Which requests did you guess correctly? Which request in Part 2 is the biggest? Which is the smallest?

LET'S TALK

Part 1 Read the list of requests. Add some ideas of your own. Think of a reason for each request.

Request	Reason	Name
lend you $250	_____	_____
help you with your homework	_____	_____
fix your bicycle	_____	_____
lend you their laptop	_____	_____
give you 25 cents	_____	_____
open the door	_____	_____
give you a lift home after school	_____	_____
lend you a jacket	_____	_____
_____		
_____		

Part 2 Ask your classmates for these favors and explain why you need them. When someone accepts, write his or her name next to the favor. You can only ask each person for one favor.

Part 3 Tell your class about two favors you asked for and two favors you agreed to do. Who had the best reasons for the favors in the list?

Conversation 2
Could you change my room?

Have you ever had problems at a hotel?
What happened? What did you do?

Class CD 2, Track 31

Uma: Excuse me.
Clerk: Yes? What can I do for you?
Uma: I just checked in, and there's a problem
with my room.
Clerk: What's the problem?
Uma: I asked for a non-smoking dorm room, but
people are smoking in there. I can't stand
it. Could you change my room, please?
Clerk: Let me see…I'm sorry, we don't have
any non-smoking dorm rooms available.
If you like, you could stay in a private
room until we have a non-smoking
available. It costs a bit more…
Uma: Yes, that'll be fine.
Clerk: OK, here's your new room key. I'll let
you know as soon as we have a bed in a
non-smoking dorm room.
Uma: Thanks for your help.

Class CD 2, Track 32
Pronunciation Focus

Notice how *can* and *can't* are
pronounced.

can /kən/   can't /kænt/
What can I do   I can't stand it.
for you?

Listen to the conversation again
and notice the pronunciation of
can and *can't*.

Student CD, Track 19

GIVE IT A TRY

1. Complaining politely

Excuse me. Sorry to bother you, but Could you help me?	I have a problem with my room.
What's the problem? What seems to be the problem?	
I asked for a non-smoking room, but I got a smoking room. I requested a room with a TV, but there isn't a TV.	

PRACTICE

Class CD 2
Track 33

Listen to the example. Student A is a hotel guest and makes three of the following complaints. Student B is the front desk clerk. Reverse roles.

1. a room with fan / no fan
2. a room with TV / no TV
3. an ocean view / a view of parking lot

4. a twin room / a double room
5. a room with a bathroom / no bathroom
6. a double room / a single room

2. Requesting action or change

Could you change my room, please?	
I'm sorry.	We can't. We don't have any other rooms available. I'll have to call the manager. There's nothing I can do. We can't now, but we can change your room tomorrow.
Thanks for your help.	

PRACTICE

Class CD 2
Track 34

Listen to the example. Student A is staying in a nice hotel, but there are a few things wrong with the room. Describe the problem and request action or change. Student B is the desk clerk. Listen to the problem and suggest a solution.

1. The room smells of cigarette smoke.
2. The room is too hot.
3. The people next door are too noisy.

4. The toilet doesn't work.
5. The window doesn't close.
6. The bed is not comfortable.

3. Accepting an apology

I'm (very) sorry about this.	That's OK. Thanks for your help. It's all right. It wasn't your fault. Don't worry about it.

PRACTICE

Role-play these problems. Student A complains, requests action, and accepts an apology. Student B asks about the problem and apologizes. Reverse roles.

Use These Words

It's broken.   There's a mistake.
     damaged.   a stain.
     dark.   a problem.
     incorrect.

LISTEN TO THIS

Class CD 2
Track 35

Part 1 Listen to two people making complaints. Where are they? What item are they talking about?

1	Where?	What?	
2	Where?	What?	

Part 2 Listen again and write the details of each problem and the result.

	Complaint	Result
1		
2		

(Student A looks at this page. Student B looks at page 114.)

Part 1 You have just arrived in Hawaii for a one-week vacation. You are at the airport and you discover that your luggage is lost. You are going to speak to the airline representative. Think of three requests for action you could make in this situation.

LOST LUGGAGE

1. _____

2. _____

3. _____

Part 2 Describe the problem to the airline representative and request action. Try to find a solution, but if it is impossible, accept an apology. Remember the following information:

- You only have one week in Hawaii, so you need the things in your suitcase right now.

- If they can't find your suitcase, you'll need some extra money to buy clothes.

- This is a terrible experience and it's going to ruin your vacation. You're very upset.

Part 3 The airline representative talks to the manager and suggests a possible solution. Listen to his or her suggestion and agree or disagree. Remember the following information:

- It's a long way to the airport from your hotel.

- The cab fare will be very expensive.

- You don't want to waste a whole day in the airport.

Now Try This

Finally, you arrive at your hotel with your suitcase. Tell your partner about your experience.

Review:
Units 7–9

**Class CD 2
Track 36**

Part 1 Listen to Joan and Kerry buying clothes for Kerry's trip to Turkey this winter. Which ones do they buy?

	Which ones?
Pants	
Sweater	
Jacket	

Part 2 Ask your partner questions about the information in the chart to find out if your partner has the same answers.

GIVE IT A TRY

Choose one of the items below. Ask the sales clerk about different sizes and colors available and the price. Buy the item. Then go back to the store again. There's something wrong with it! Complain politely and ask for a refund or an exchange. Then reverse roles.

**Class CD 2
Track 37**

Part 1 Listen to a man and a woman ordering food in a restaurant. Write *M* next to the food the man orders. Write *W* next to the food the woman orders.

Part 2 Ask your partner questions about the information in the menu to find out if your partner has the same answers.

Lunch Special

Entrees
____ New York Steak
____ Lobster Tails
____ Salmon Teriyaki
____ Barbecued Chicken

Side Dishes
Potato
____ mashed ____ boiled ____ baked
Vegetable
____ broccoli ____ asparagus ____ carrots

Appetizers
____ Soup or ____ Salad
____ French ____ Italian ____ Blue Cheese

Desserts
____ Ice Cream ____ Cake ____ Fresh Fruit

Beverages
____ Coffee ____ Iced Coffee
____ Tea ____ Iced Tea ____ Herbal Tea

GIVE IT A TRY

What is your favorite dish? What are the main ingredients? How is it cooked? What does it taste like? Walk around the room and describe the dish to another student. Your classmates will try to guess what it is.

Favorite food	
What are the main ingredients?	
How is it cooked?	
What does it taste like?	

LISTEN TO THIS UNIT 9

Class CD 2
Track 38

Part 1 Listen to these three conversations. What is the problem? What is the result?

	Problem	Result
1		
2		
3		

Part 2 Ask your partner about each of the situations above to find out if your partner has the same answers.

GIVE IT A TRY

Work in groups. Read the list of items. Write one reason why you want to borrow each item. Take turns asking to borrow things. Explain your reason.

a book about Egypt   a sleeping bag   a ladder   some drinking glasses and plates
a hammer   a CD player   a camera   a backpack

Unit 10

Conversation 1
Where are you from?

What questions do you usually ask when you meet a person for the first time?

CONSIDER THIS

Moving Day

There's only one day each year when people in Montreal, Canada, can move from an old apartment to a new one. Each July 1st, about 650,000 people move. Why can't they move another day? No one's sure, but it's the law!

● How many times have you moved to a different house? To a different city?

Class CD 2, Track 39

Glenn:	So Sabrina, where are you from?
Sabrina:	I'm from Canada originally.
Glenn:	Really? That's cool. I love visiting Canada! Where were you born?
Sabrina:	I was born in Montreal.
Glenn:	When did you come to Los Angeles then?
Sabrina:	Well, my family moved here when I was ten.
Glenn:	Oh, did you go to school here?
Sabrina:	Yeah, I went to middle school here, but I went to high school in Pasadena.
Glenn:	Did you go to college right after high school?
Sabrina:	Actually, I didn't. I traveled for a while in Europe, and I lived in France for six months.
Glenn:	Cool. When was that?
Sabrina:	Let's see…. That was almost two years ago! I can't believe it's been that long!
Glenn:	I bet it was a fascinating experience. What did you do while you were there?
Sabrina:	Oh, nothing that interesting…I just studied French. Anyway, that's enough about me! How about you? Were you born in Los Angeles?

Student CD, Track 20

GIVE IT A TRY

1. Giving and getting personal information (1)

Where are you from?	(I'm from) Canada (originally).
Where were you born?	(I was born in) Montreal.
Were you born in Los Angeles? here? there?	Yes, I was. No, I was born in Canada.

PRACTICE

Class CD 2 Track 40

Listen to the example. Then ask your classmates where they are from and where they were born. Make a list.

2. Giving and getting personal information (2)

Did you go to school here?
Yes, I went to middle school here, but I went to high school in Pasadena. No, I went to school in Boston.
Did you go to college right after high school?
Yes, I started college right away. No, I traveled in Europe for a while.

PRACTICE 1

Class CD 2 Track 41

Listen to the example. Now imagine you are at a party in Seoul. Ask and answer questions using the information below.

Student A's questions
1. high school / here?
2. college / here?
3. get a job after college?
4. work in Oman?

Student B's answers
1. yes / college, too
2. no / Kyongju
3. no / lived in Oman for a while
4. no / studied Arabic

PRACTICE 2

Ask your partner these questions about his or her life. Then add your own questions. Reverse roles.

1. grow up / go to elementary school / high school around here?
2. study English / do sports in elementary or high school ?
3. go to college right after high school?

3. Being specific

> I traveled in Europe for a while.
>
> Did you? And when was that?
>
> That was almost two years ago / in 2004.
>   when I was eighteen / right after high school.

PRACTICE 1

Class CD 2 Track 42

Listen to the example. Then look at Sabrina's time line below. Imagine you are Sabrina and your partner is Glenn. Sabrina will make statements about her life. Glenn will ask for more specific information. Reverse roles.

Sabrina: I went to elementary school in Montreal.
Glenn: Did you? When was that?
Sabrina: When I was 6. / In 1992.

SABRINA'S TIME LINE

YEAR	1992	1996	2000	2004 Sept.–Dec.	2005 Jan.–June	2005 Sept.–now
AGE	6	10	14	18	18	19
	Elementary School in Montreal	Middle School in L.A.	High School in Pasadena	Traveling in Europe	Living in France	College in L.A.

PRACTICE 2

Fill in the time line of your life and place five important events on it. Tell your partner about it. Answer his or her questions about when each event happened and how old you were. Reverse roles.

> **Use These Words**
> grow up
> attend / go to (school)
> move
> leave home
> come back
> graduate from
> work part-time / full-time

YOUR TIME LINE

YEAR						
AGE						

LISTEN TO THIS

Class CD 2
Track 43

Part 1 Listen to Glenn tell Sabrina about his life. The following are some of the places he has lived. Number them in the correct order.

___ Hawaii ___ Seattle ___ Saudi Arabia ___ Munich
___ Tokyo ___ Alaska ___ Los Angeles

Part 2 Listen again and fill in the events in Glenn's time line.

Glenn's Time Line				After high school
2 years old	In 1991	10 years old	In 2003	

Part 3 Tell your partner about Glenn's life. Your partner will ask for more specific information. Answer his or her questions.

LET'S TALK

Part 1 Think of an important or unusual event in your life and write it down on a piece of paper. Don't put your name on the paper.

Part 2 Give that piece of paper to your teacher or group leader. Then pick out a different piece of paper from the pile. Ask your classmates questions to try to find the person who wrote the information on your new piece of paper.

Part 3 When you find the person who wrote the information, ask them for more specific information about the event. Then write down their answers.

Conversation 2
How long did you do that?

What questions would you ask someone you haven't seen in a long time?

Class CD 2, Track 44

Sabrina: Marie! Is that you? It's been so long. How are you? What are you doing these days?

Marie: Hi, Sabrina! Good to see you! You're not going to believe this, but I'm actually a chef!

Sabrina: You're kidding! You've always hated cooking!

Marie: I know! I used to hate it, but now I love it.

Sabrina: What made you change your mind?

Marie: Well, it was when I tried vegetarian food. Before that, I used to cook really boring things, but vegetarian food was so much fun to cook.

Sabrina: I still can't believe it! So, where did you go to cooking school?

Marie: I went to San Francisco to study.

Sabrina: Really? How long did you stay there?

Marie: I was there for about two years.

Sabrina: And what did you do after that?

Marie: Well, then I came back here. I got a job as a junior chef here in L.A. because I was a little homesick.

Sabrina: That means we can hang out! So where is your restaurant? Can I book a table for this weekend?

Class CD 2, Track 45
Pronunciation Focus

Did you is often pronounced *didya* in spoken conversation.

Did you go to cooking school?
How long did you stay there?
And what did you do after that?

Listen to the conversation again and notice the pronunciation of *did you*.

Student CD, Track 21

GIVE IT A TRY

Marie Sims

Sept. 1999	entered Pasadena High School
June 2003	graduated Pasadena High School
June– Sept. 2003	chef's assistant, Blue Cuisine, San Francisco
July– Aug. 2003	server, Paris Bistro, Long Beach
Sept. 2003	entered California School of Cooking, San Francisco
May 2005	graduated California School of Cooking, San Francisco
June 2005	returned to L.A.
June– July 2005	part-time junior chef, The Vegetarian Garden, L.A.
July 2005– now	full-time junior chef, The Vegetarian Garden, L.A.

1. Discussing length of time

How long did you	go to Pasadena High School? stay in California? live there?
I went there I was there I stayed there	for four years. between 1998 and 2000. from 1998 to 2000.

PRACTICE 1

Class CD 2 Track 46

Listen to the example. Then look at Marie's resume and imagine your partner is Marie. Ask about three of these things. Reverse roles.

Student A asks

1. go to Pasadena High
2. work as a server
3. go to cooking school

Student B asks

1. work as a chef's assistant
2. live in San Francisco
3. work part-time at The Vegetarian Garden

PRACTICE 2

Ask your partner about the time line he or she made on page 82.

2. Asking *What next?*

What did you do	after high school? after leaving San Francisco? after that? then?	Well, then I came back here. I worked as a server for six weeks.

PRACTICE 1

Class CD 2 Track 47

Listen to the example. Your partner is Marie. Ask her about her education and work history. Reverse roles.

PRACTICE 2

Ask your partner about events on his or her time line. Reverse roles.

3. Describing changes

> I used to hate cooking, but now I love it.
> I used to cook really boring things, but now I don't.
>
> What made you change your mind?
>
> It was when I tried vegetarian food.

PRACTICE

Listen to the example. Work in groups. Tell the other group members three things that used to be true for you. Say how they have changed. Reverse roles.

| music | food | clothes | hobbies |
| books | sports | TV shows | school subjects |

LISTEN TO THIS

Part 1 Sting is the name of a popular English musician, guitarist, and singer. Listen to a short description of his career. Fill in the chart below.

| Born: | Where? | | When? |

Date

1971–74: _____

1977: _____

1984: _____

1985: _____

1989: _____

2003: _____

Part 2 Listen again and write notes on the changes in Sting's life.

	Then	Now
Occupation		
Lifestyle		
Music groups		
Type of music		
Hometown		
Interests		

Part 3 Talk to your partner about Sting's life. How is his life now different from his life when he was young?

Part 1 You are a career counselor. You are going to help your partner to choose a career. You are going to fill out the form below with your partner's information. Read the form carefully and think of what questions you will need to ask. Write down three questions:

1. _____

2. _____

3. _____

Part 2 Now interview your partner about his or her personal information and suggest a career. Reverse roles.

Name: _____

Date of Birth: _____   Place of Birth: _____

EDUCATION

Name and Location	From	To	Subjects/Interests
Elementary School			
High School			
College			
Other Education or Training			

EMPLOYMENT

Name and Location	From	To	Subjects/Interests
Company			
Company			
Company			

Activities, Interests, and Hobbies: _____

Recommended Career: _____

Now Try This

Think of another career that might be good for you. Make a list of reasons why.

Conversation 1
Have you ever been to Japan?

Think of a place you have visited on vacation. Describe it to a friend.

CONSIDER THIS

The world's largest country

Russia—its total size is over 17,000,000 square km. More than 143 million people live there.

- What interesting facts do you know about your country?
- About another country?
- What fact would you like to know about another country?

Class CD 2, Track 50

Annuar:	Have you ever been to Japan? I'm going in the fall.
Taka:	Yeah, I've been there twice.
Annuar:	Really? Tell me about it. What's it like?
Taka:	Oh, it's fantastic.
Annuar:	Where did you go?
Taka:	On my first trip I went to Tokyo, and on my second I visited Kyoto.
Annuar:	What did you think of Tokyo?
Taka:	Very big and exciting, but really crowded, too.
Annuar:	Yeah, I've seen pictures of the crowded subways!
Taka:	And the restaurants are excellent…but they're kind of expensive.
Annuar:	And how about Kyoto?
Taka:	Kyoto is lovely. It's a very historic city, very peaceful and quiet.
Annuar:	Wow, that sounds great…what about the weather?
Taka:	Well, the first time I went was in August, so it was really hot and humid. But the second time was in October and it was great. Warm and sunny, but not humid.
Annuar:	Sounds perfect! I'm really looking forward to my trip.

Student CD, Track 22

GIVE IT A TRY

1. Asking about past experiences

| Have you ever | been to Japan? |
| | gone to a foreign country? |

Yes,	I've been there twice.	No, never.
	I was there last summer.	No, but I'd like to (go there).
	the last time was in April.	
	several times.	

PRACTICE 1

Class CD 2
Track 51 Listen to the example. Then ask your partner if they have ever done four of the things in the list. Reverse roles.

gone to / a foreign country   eaten / a strange food   drunk / a strange drink

slept / in the open air   climbed / a mountain   swum / in a waterfall

PRACTICE 2

Think of three more questions. Ask your partner and two other classmates.

2. Asking for a description or opinion

What do you think of Tokyo?	It's very big and exciting, but it's crowded.
What is Kyoto like?	It's very historic, and it's peaceful.
What is the weather like?	It's really hot and humid.
How is the weather?	It's usually humid in August.

PRACTICE

Class CD 2
Track 52 Listen to the example. Talk about these cities. Use the adjectives next to each picture.

① Tokyo

crowded

noisy

exciting

hot and humid in the summer

② Montreal

clean / quiet

attractive

freezing cold and snowy in the winter

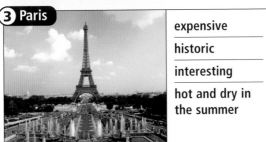

③ Paris

expensive

historic

interesting

hot and dry in the summer

④ Bangkok

cheap

noisy

exciting

dry and warm in the winter

3. Asking for more details

What is the food like? How is the food?	It's hot and spicy.
What are the restaurants like? How are the restaurants?	They're pretty expensive.

PRACTICE

Class CD 2
Track 53

Listen to the example. Then choose a town or city that you know. Your partner will ask you questions about each of the following topics. Reverse roles.

the hotels   the stores

the downtown   the food

the people   the weather

the nightlife   the public transportation

Use These Words

spicy	delicious
old-fashioned	modern
exciting	awful
terrible	attractive
interesting	scenic
kind	friendly
run-down	comfortable
quite	really
very	not very

LISTEN TO THIS

Class CD 2
Track 54

Part 1 Minako has just come back from vacation in San Francisco. She is telling her friend Lynn about it. What does she think about San Francisco?

Part 2 Now listen and write down Minako's opinions about each topic.

Minako's opinions	
The city	
The transportation	
The restaurants	
The hotel	

Part 3 What did Minako like about San Francisco? What did she dislike?

LET'S TALK

Part 1 Choose one city that you have visited. Write your opinions in the chart.

Part 2 Ask four classmates for their opinions of the city you have chosen. Find out if they agree or disagree with your opinion. (If they have not visited the city, you may ask them what they *think* it is like.)

Name of town or city: _____

	Your opinion	Student 1	Student 2	Student 3	Student 4
city					
food					
people					
weather					
transportation					
nightlife					
stores					

Part 3 Give a report to your group on what you found out. How many people have visited your city? What were their opinions? Do you agree or disagree?

Conversation 2
Which city did you like better?

What is your favorite city? Describe it to a friend.

Class CD 2, Track 55

Taka: Oh, hi, Anna. When did you get back from Canada?

Anna: The day before yesterday. I only visited Montreal and Ottawa, but I had a great time.

Taka: Which city did you like better?

Anna: That's hard to say…I think Ottawa is prettier. It has better sight-seeing, too, but Montreal is more exciting. It has better shopping, and the stores are cheaper and more interesting.

Taka: Which one has better nightlife?

Anna: Oh, Montreal, for sure. It definitely has more restaurants and clubs. In fact, they say Montreal is the most exciting city in Canada.

Taka: Really? Well, I've always wanted to see Vancouver. I've heard it has the most beautiful scenery.

Student CD, Track 23

Class CD 2, Track 56
Pronunciation Focus

Notice the [r] sound at the end of these words.

better   more
prettier   cheaper

Notice how the [r] sound at the end of a word is linked to a vowel at the beginning of the next word.

more͜exciting   cheaper͜and

Listen to the conversation again and notice the [r] sounds.

GIVE IT A TRY

1. Comparing places (1)

> Which city do you like better, Montreal or Ottawa?
>
> I think Ottawa is prettier, but Montreal is more exciting.

Use These Words

Short adjectives:
older, newer, quieter, cleaner, cheaper, busier, prettier, hotter, bigger
Exception: better

Long adjectives:
more expensive, more interesting, more attractive, more exciting, more crowded

PRACTICE 1

Class CD 2 Track 57 Listen to the example. Then take turns asking about the pairs of cities below.

1. Montreal / Ottawa
2. Sydney / Melbourne
3. London / Paris
4. Hong Kong / Taipei
5. Kuala Lumpur / Singapore
6. Seoul / Pusan
7. Bangkok / Chiang Mai
8. San Francisco / Los Angeles

PRACTICE 2

Work in groups. Think of two cities in your country or in another country, and compare them. Use the words in the box.

2. Comparing places (2)

Which	city place	has	nicer more interesting better	weather? sight-seeing? shopping?	Ottawa. There are more museums. Montreal. The stores are more interesting. My hometown has nicer weather. It's always warm and sunny.

PRACTICE

Class CD 2 Track 58 Listen to the example. Then choose a city or region that you have visited. Your partner will ask you to compare it to your hometown. Reverse roles.

Ask which place has:

1. nicer weather
2. newer buildings
3. cheaper restaurants
4. bigger hotels
5. better sight-seeing
6. better transportation
7. friendlier people
8. your idea _____

3. Comparing places (3)

Which city is the most exciting?	Montreal is the most exciting city in Canada.
Which city has the best scenery?	Vancouver. It has the most beautiful scenery in Canada.

PRACTICE 1

Class CD 2 Track 59

Listen to the example. Then make a list of five main cities in your country (or neighborhoods in your city). Work in groups. Discuss what is best about each of them. Talk about: entertainment, scenery, shopping, nightlife, sight-seeing, restaurants, people, and food.

PRACTICE 2

Report to the class on the opinions of your group. See if your classmates agree or disagree.

LISTEN TO THIS

Part 1 What do you know about Thailand? What do you think about: the hotels, the sight-seeing, the people, the food, the shopping, the weather? Make a list of possible adjectives to describe each topic.

Class CD 2 Track 60

Part 2 Dina is going on a trip to Thailand. She is asking her friend for some advice on where to go and what to do. Listen to the conversation and write the information next to each place on the map.

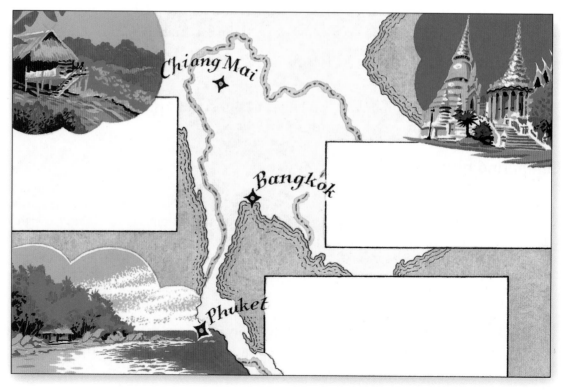

Part 3 Which places do you think are most popular with tourists? Why?

(Student A looks at this page. Student B looks at page 115.)

Part 1 Read the information about Hong Kong and Rio de Janeiro. Make a list of adjectives you could use to compare these two cities.

_____   _____   _____

_____   _____   _____

Part 2 Compare the cities using the adjectives in your list. Tell your partner which city you think is more interesting to visit and why. Your partner also has some information about two different cities. Ask questions and find out which city is more interesting to visit and why.

Rio de Janeiro

Restaurants: Open air food markets. Prices from $5 per person.

Nightlife: Folk music, Latin dancing, Carnival.

Sight-seeing: Copacabana Beach, art galleries.

Shopping: Boutiques for swimwear.

HONG KONG

Restaurants: Choose from hundreds of restaurants: Chinese, Japanese, Thai, Vietnamese, French, Italian, and Indian. Prices from $20 per person.

Nightlife: Classical music, concerts, ballet, opera (western and Chinese).

Sight-seeing: Best views of the city from Victoria Peak, take a trip in a dhow, wish for good luck at a temple.

Shopping: Best fashion bargains in Asia, designer names at half the price, handmade tailored suits and shirts.

Part 3 Fill out the chart for all four cities.

Best...	Food	Sight-seeing	Nightlife	Shopping
Hong Kong				
Rio de Janeiro				

Now Try This

Imagine you are planning a trip around the world with your friend. You can visit four cities anywhere in the world. Which cities would you visit and why? Tell the class about your plan.

Unit 12

Conversation 1
What are you going to do?

Who do you usually ask for help and advice? Do you always follow their advice?

CONSIDER THIS

Gap year

About 60,000 young British people take a year off—a gap year—after high school, before university. What do they do?

—travel
—language study
—volunteer work
—learn a new sport
—informal study

- Would you like to have a gap year (or did you)?
- What would you like to do with a year off?

Class CD 2, Track 61

Counselor:	Only three more months to go! What are you going to do after you graduate, Sakura?
Sakura:	I'm going to go to graduate school in Ohio.
Counselor:	What are you going to study?
Sakura:	I'm planning to study architecture.
Counselor:	That's a good field. And what about you, Sun-hee?
Sun-hee:	I'm planning to work in my father's company next year.
Counselor:	And what are you doing after that?
Sun-hee:	I'm going back to school to get my degree in business.
Counselor:	That's a great plan. How about you, Miguel?
Miguel:	I'm not going to get a job right away. I'm going to spend some time traveling in Europe.
Counselor:	Sounds great! How long will you be there?
Miguel:	Well, I'm leaving in June and I'll be there about six months.
Counselor:	Which countries will you visit?
Miguel:	Maybe France and Spain. I haven't decided yet.

1. Discussing future plans (1)

What do you plan to do	after you graduate?
What are you going to do	in the fall?
What are you planning to do	next year?

I'm (not) going to	get a job right away.
I'm (not) planning to	travel in Europe.
I haven't decided yet.	

PRACTICE

Class CD 2 Track 62

Listen to the example. Then ask your partner about his or her future plans using the information below. Fill in the blank with your own idea.

1. after school / work tonight
2. the day after tomorrow
3. this weekend

4. for your next vacation
5. after you graduate
6. your idea _____

2. Discussing future plans (2)

What are you doing after that?	I'm going back to school.
	I'm going to travel for a year.
	I'm not sure yet.

PRACTICE 1

Class CD 2 Track 63

Listen to the example. Then ask your partner what he or she is doing at these times. Use the information in the pictures. Reverse roles.

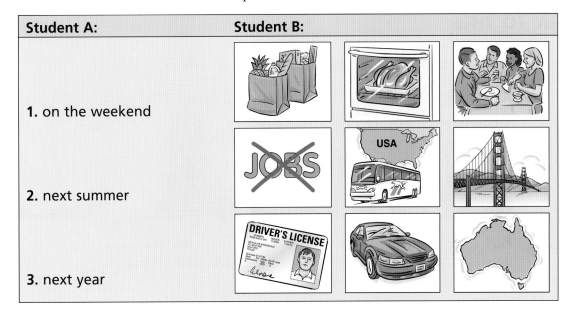

Student A:

1. on the weekend

2. next summer

3. next year

Student B:

PRACTICE 2

Ask your partner about these times again. This time, give answers about yourself.

3. Discussing future plans (3)

When will you be in Europe?	I'll be there | in June. | on June 17.
How long will you be there?	(I'll be there) for six months.
What countries will you visit?	France and Italy.
What will you do there?	I'm going to learn about European art.

Romantic Capitals of Europe IN *15* DAYS

MONDAY JUNE 17, Early morning arrival in Paris, three nights in this romantic city: Visit the Palace of Versailles and the Eiffel Tower.

THURSDAY JUNE 20, Overnight to Rome: Visit the monuments of ancient Rome, candlelit dinner included.

FRIDAY JUNE 21, Vienna, city of romantic music, visit Schonbrunn Palace, try Vienna's famous pastry shops, tickets to the opera included.

SUNDAY JUNE 23, Historic Prague: Visit the Castle, Mozart's opera house, and take a boat trip on the Vltava River.

WEDNESDAY JUNE 26, Trendy Berlin: Visit the latest art galleries and the new Parliament building.

FRIDAY JUNE 28, London: city of fashion, fun, and shopping: Oxford Street, Harrods, and Kensington High Street.

SUNDAY JUNE 30, Early morning flight home.

PRACTICE

Class CD 2
Track 64 Listen to the example. You have booked a trip to Europe. Your partner will ask you questions with *When…?*, *How long…?*, and *What…?* Look at the schedule and answer the questions. Reverse roles.

LISTEN TO THIS

Part 1 What do you know about Egypt? Match the words with the pictures.

___ Pyramid   ___ felucca   ___ sphinx   ___ camel

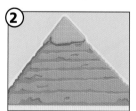

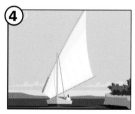

Class CD 2
Track 65 *Part 2* Irene is planning to go to Egypt for her winter vacation. Listen to the details of her trip and fill in the missing information. If Irene decides *not* to do something, write ✗ next to it.

Day 1	Day 2	Day 3	Day 4	Day 5	Day 6
Arrive in Cairo					
Whole day free					

LET'S TALK

Part 1 Read the list of possible future projects and choose one that you would like to do in the next five years (or add your own idea).

- ☐ write a book
- ☐ record a CD
- ☐ travel around the world
- ☐ build a house
- ☐ design a new kind of school
- ☐ produce a TV program
- ☐ design a new product
- ☐ start a community service project

- ☐ make a film
- ☐ design a fashion store
- ☐ start a company
- ☐ design a website
- ☐ create a new invention
- ☐ start a new magazine
- ☐ raise money to help people
- ☐ your idea _____

Part 2 Find someone in your class or group who has chosen the same plan. Discuss your plan together and try to agree on the details. Ask questions with *Where...?*, *When...?*, and *How long...?* Think about what you will do after achieving this goal.

Our Plan:	Picture
We are planning to	
Where?	
When? How long? After?	

Part 3 Prepare a report for the class on your project. Answer questions from the class.

Conversation 2
What do you want to do?

What goals do you have for the future? What do you hope your future will be like?

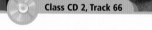

Class CD 2, Track 66

Sun-hee: What do you want to do in the future, Miguel?

Miguel: I don't know what kind of job I want, but I know I want to study languages.

Sakura: That sounds interesting. Which languages do you want to study?

Miguel: French and German. What do you think you'll do, Sakura?

Sakura: I want to be an architect. After I graduate, I hope to get a job back in my hometown and settle down. I'd like to design houses and schools there.

Miguel: That sounds like a good plan.

Sun-hee: I'm planning to study business, but I'm not sure if that's right for me. I might take some time off so I can decide what I want to do.

Sakura: What do you think you'll do instead?

Sun-hee: I'm not sure. Maybe I'll try something completely different.

Student CD, Track 25

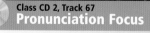

Class CD 2, Track 67
Pronunciation Focus

In spoken conversation, the words *what do you* are often linked together.

What do you want to do?
What do you think you'll do?

Listen to the conversation again and notice the pronunciation of *what do you.*

GIVE IT A TRY

1. Discussing goals

What do you want to do? What would you like to do?	I want to I'd like to	study languages.
That sounds interesting. Which languages do you want to study?	I'd like to learn French and Spanish.	

PRACTICE

Class CD 2
 Track 68

Listen to the example. Your partner will ask you about three things you want to do next year. Use the pictures below for ideas. Add some ideas of your own. Then your partner will ask for more information. Reverse roles.

2. Discussing hopes

What do you hope	you'll do (next year)? to do? will happen?	I hope	I'll get a job. I get a job. to get a job.

PRACTICE

Class CD 2
 Track 69

Listen to the example. Then fill in the chart with your information. Work in groups to discuss your future hopes for next year, the next five years, and the next ten years.

Use These Words

try	design
build	create
start	invent
buy	meet
settle down	

Next year	In the next five years	In the next ten years

3. Discussing possibilities

What do you think you'll do after you graduate?	I might take some time off. Maybe I'll try something completely different. I haven't made up my mind yet.

PRACTICE 1

Class CD 2 Track 70

Listen to the example. Then discuss some possible choices for future plans with your partner. Answer each other's questions and reverse roles.

1. which subjects / take / next semester
2. which sports / do / next semester
3. where / live / next year
4. where / go / on your next vacation
5. what / do / on your next vacation
6. what kind of job / apply for / after college
7. what / do / after you graduate
8. your idea _____

PRACTICE 2

Think of some more questions to ask about the future. Try to use *which, where, when, who,* and *how long.*

LISTEN TO THIS

Part 1 Look at the picture of Alexi and Ivan. They are college students now, but what do you think they will be like in ten years?

Class CD 2 Track 71

Part 2 Listen to Alexi and his friend Ivan discussing their lives ten years from now. Check (✔) the things they are sure about, and mark the things they are not sure about with an ✗.

	Alexi	Ivan
Job		
Home		
Friends		
Family		
Personality		
Appearance		

Part 3 Compare Alexi and Ivan's answers. What kind of a person is Alexi? What kind of a person is Ivan?

Part 1 You are going to help your partner visualize his or her goals in the next five years. Read the questionnaire.

Part 2 Ask your partner the following questions. Listen carefully to his or her answers and choose the best number. Finally, add up the score and tell your partner the result.

How do you see yourself in five years?

Answer the questions by circling 1 to 5.

1 What kind of job do you think you will have?

| CREATIVE | 1 | 2 | 3 | 4 | 5 | RELIABLE |

2 What kind of friends do you think you will have?

| ENERGETIC | 1 | 2 | 3 | 4 | 5 | RELAXED |

3 What kind of house do you think you will live in?

| UNUSUAL | 1 | 2 | 3 | 4 | 5 | COMFORTABLE |

4 What kind of clothes do you think you will wear?

| FASHIONABLE | 1 | 2 | 3 | 4 | 5 | CLASSIC |

5 What kind of vacations do you think you will have?

| ADVENTUROUS | 1 | 2 | 3 | 4 | 5 | RELAXING |

6 Do you think your appearance will be the same or different?

| COMPLETELY DIFFERENT | 1 | 2 | 3 | 4 | 5 | THE SAME |

7 Do you think your personality will be the same or different?

| COMPLETELY DIFFERENT | 1 | 2 | 3 | 4 | 5 | THE SAME |

8 What values do you think will be most important to you?

| SUCCESS AT WORK | 1 | 2 | 3 | 4 | 5 | PERSONAL LIFE |

SCORE

1-10 Ambitous:
You'll take risks in order to achieve your goal. You like change and are willing to try new things. You aren't tied to friends, things, or places.

20-30 Cautious:
You'll try to achieve your goals without taking any risks. You might have to make some compromises along the way. Continuity is important to you.

30-40 Easygoing:
You'll be happy whatever the future brings. You like a peaceful stress-free life.

Part 3 Now reverse roles. Your partner will help you to visualize your future. Answer his or her questions. How are you and your partner different or similar in your view of the future?

Now Try This

Use the information in the questionnaire to describe your partner's ideal lifestyle.

Review:
Units 10–12

Class CD 2 Track 72

Part 1 Listen to the biography of this famous man. Write the missing information in the chart. Who is he?

1. Born where? _____ 2. When? _____
3. _____ he went to university.
4. _____ he joined the African National Congress.
5. _____ he was in prison.
6. _____ he started writing his autobiography.
7. _____ he became president of South Africa.
8. _____ his autobiography *Long Walk to Freedom* was published.
9. _____ he retired from public life.

Part 2 Ask your partner questions about the information above to find out if your partner has the same answers.

GIVE IT A TRY

Think of a famous person (or use the information above). Imagine that you are a journalist and you are going to interview this person. Ask questions about important events in his or her life. How has his or her life changed? Role-play the conversation with a partner. Then reverse roles.

LISTEN TO THIS **UNIT 11**

Class CD 2 Track 73

Part 1 Listen to Ron and Sachiko talk about Sachiko's trip to Europe. Write the adjectives next to each city.

Vienna	
Prague	
Budapest	

Part 2 Ask your partner questions about Sachiko's opinions to find out if your partner has the same answers.

GIVE IT A TRY

Work in a group of four students. Ask Student A if he or she has ever done three of these things. Student A will give two true answers and one false answer. The group can ask five more questions to find out which sentence was true and which was false. If they do not guess, Student A scores one point.

LISTEN TO THIS UNIT 12

Class CD 2 Track 74 *Part 1* Ben and Jill are high school friends who will be graduating soon. They are talking to each other about the future. Listen and fill in the missing information in the chart.

	Ben	Jill
After high school		
After college		
Future hopes		

Part 2 Ask your partner questions about Ben and Jill's plans to find out if your partner has the same answers.

GIVE IT A TRY

Work in a group of four students. Imagine that your group has won $500,000 in the lottery. How will you spend the money? Make a list of all the things you will do. Will you use the money for yourself, your school, or your community? Tell the class what you are going to do with the money.

You	Your school	Your community

(Students C and D look at this page. Students A and B look at page 9.)

Part 1 Students C and D will interview Students A and B together. Complete the missing information for Students A and B.

Student C: You are Amy Jiang.

Student D: You are Toshihiko Matsuda.

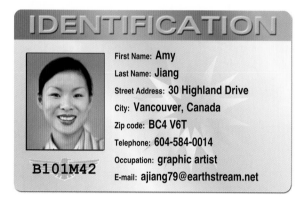

IDENTIFICATION

First Name: **Amy**
Last Name: **Jiang**
Street Address: **30 Highland Drive**
City: **Vancouver, Canada**
Zip code: **BC4 V6T**
Telephone: **604-584-0014**
Occupation: **graphic artist**
E-mail: **ajiang79@earthstream.net**

B101M42

IDENTIFICATION

First Name: **Toshihiko**
Last Name: **Matsuda**
Street Address: **214 Madison Avenue**
City: **New York, U.S.**
Zip code: **10016**
Telephone: **212-726-5309**
Occupation: **journalist**
E-mail: **tmatsuda30@yahos.com**

F456R94

Write Student B's information here:

Write Student A's information here:

IDENTIFICATION

First Name: _____
Last Name: _____
Street Address: _____
City: _____
Zip code: _____
Telephone: _____
Occupation: _____
E-mail: _____

IDENTIFICATION

First Name: _____
Last Name: _____
Street Address: _____
City: _____
Zip code: _____
Telephone: _____
Occupation: _____
E-mail: _____

Part 2 Now show your page to Students A and B. Is all the information the same? Ask questions to check spelling.

Part 3 Imagine all four of you are at a party. Introduce yourselves to each other. Say your names, where you live, and what you do.

Now Try This

Walk around the class and introduce yourself again. Use your own personal information. Make a list of everyone you meet with all their information.

(Student B looks at this page. Student A looks at page 17.)

Part 1 Look at Sally's family tree. Look at each family member and think of how you can describe each person's age, appearance, hair, clothing, and family relationship.

Part 2 Your partner also has a family tree. There are ten differences between the two family trees. Ask questions to find the differences. Don't look at your partner's page.

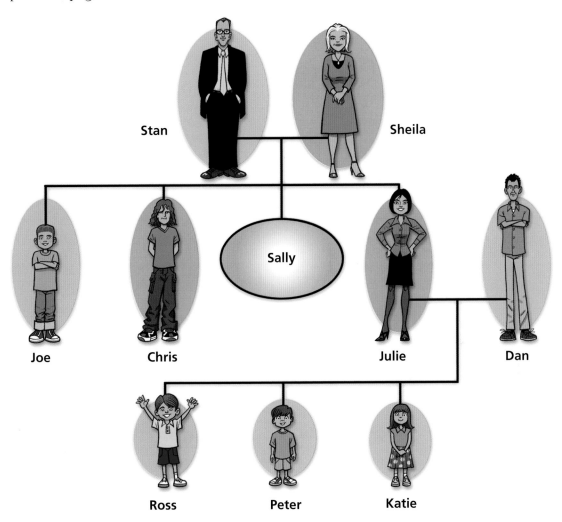

Part 3 Write sentences about the differences between the two family trees.

Example: My tree has two younger brothers, but my partner's tree has…

Now Try This

Write sentences about the differences between your family and your partner's family.

(Student B looks at this page. Student A looks at page 25.)

Part 1 Look at the picture. Do you know what these inventions are for? How can you describe each one?

Part 2 Describe your four inventions to your partner. Where is the object? What does it look like? Your partner will draw the object on his or her picture and try to guess what it is used for. Reverse roles. (Remember: Don't say the name of the object or what it is used for. Your partner will guess.)

projector
document holder
speakerphone
mouse

Now Try This

Think of a new gadget (a real or imaginary one!) for your home or for your office. What does it look like? What is it used for? Describe it to your partner. Your partner will try to guess what it is.

(Student B looks at this page. Student A looks at page 35.)

Part 1 Look at your map. Which buildings aren't labeled? Write two questions about them and then ask your partner.

1. _____

2. _____

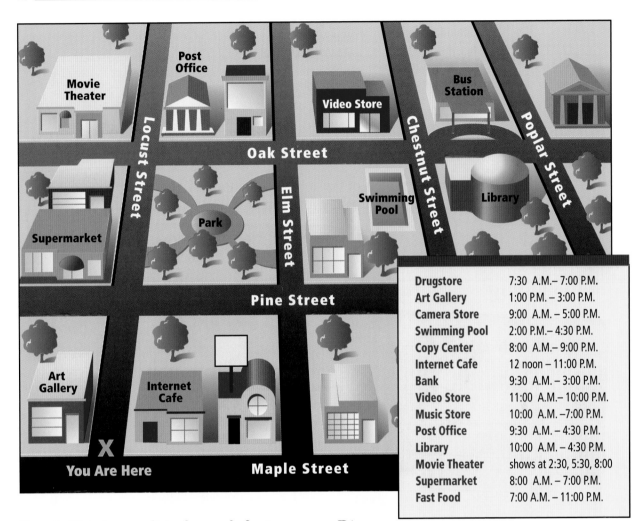

Drugstore 7:30 A.M.– 7:00 P.M.
Art Gallery 1:00 P.M. – 3:00 P.M.
Camera Store 9:00 A.M. – 5:00 P.M.
Swimming Pool 2:00 P.M.– 4:30 P.M.
Copy Center 8:00 A.M.– 9:00 P.M.
Internet Cafe 12 noon – 11:00 P.M.
Bank 9:30 A.M. – 3:00 P.M.
Video Store 11:00 A.M.– 10:00 P.M.
Music Store 10:00 A.M. –7:00 P.M.
Post Office 9:30 A.M. – 4:30 P.M.
Library 10:00 A.M. – 4:30 P.M.
Movie Theater shows at 2:30, 5:30, 8:00
Supermarket 8:00 A.M. – 7:00 P.M.
Fast Food 7:00 A.M. – 11:00 P.M.

Part 2 This is your list of errands for tomorrow. Discuss your route on the map with your partner. Number the places on the map in the order that you visit them, and write the time next to each one. Remember to allow time for each errand.

visit the new art exhibition
rent a video
buy some milk
send a package
send an e-mail

(together with your partner)
have lunch
see a movie
go swimming

Now Try This

Draw an X somewhere on your map. That is your home. Tell your partner how to get there from another point on the map. Your partner will tell you how to get to his or her home from your home. Then compare maps.

(Student B looks at this page. Student A looks at page 43.)

Part 1 You are Joe. Here are your likes and dislikes. Your partner is Katya. Find out which likes and dislikes you share and write them in the chart below.

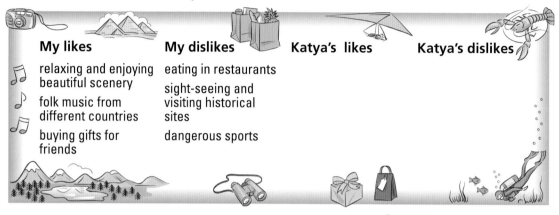

My likes	My dislikes	Katya's likes	Katya's dislikes
relaxing and enjoying beautiful scenery	eating in restaurants		
folk music from different countries	sight-seeing and visiting historical sites		
buying gifts for friends	dangerous sports		

Part 2 Choose which of these three vacations would be ideal for you and your partner.

CHIANG MAI

Enjoy the beautiful animals and natural scenery of the jungle, trekking and climbing in the nearby hills.

Visit ancient temples, and learn about yoga and meditation.

Unique handmade goods—choose from hand-woven cloth, paintings, statues, and silver jewelry.

Rio de Janeiro

Enjoy the world's most multi-cultural city. The music and dancing of Carnival time in Rio is an experience you will never forget.

Exotic food from all over South America—shrimp, okra, and spicy chili from the north, mangoes and guavas from the south.

Exciting scuba diving and snorkeling in the beautiful ocean's reefs and caves. Create your own underwater adventure.

ISTANBUL

A HISTORY LOVER'S PARADISE— Greek and Roman ruins, palaces and castles of the Ottoman emperors.

SPEND A DAY IN THE BAZAAR— shopping for silk rugs, silver jewelry, or leather jackets.

EAT IN A TRADITIONAL TURKISH RESTAURANT— have stuffed eggplant, dumplings with yogurt, and famous Turkish pastries for dessert.

Now Try This

Make a list of things you plan to do on your three-day vacation. Plan your schedule for each day.

(Student B looks at this page. Student A looks at page 51.)

Part 1 You are going to visit your friend's hometown this weekend. Talk with him or her on the phone and plan your daily schedule. Try to do as many things as you can. Talk about the time and day you will go to each place or event. You will arrive at 7:00 P.M. on Friday night and leave at 4:00 P.M. on Sunday.

You also found the following information on the Internet.

Around Town

AROUND TOWN EVENTS

HOME

NEXT WEEK

THIS WEEKEND

Pink Elephant
Thai restaurant
Lunch 12–3,
Dinner 5–midnight

The Lions v. the Eagles
Soccer game
starts Saturday 4:00 P.M.

Indian Art and Music
Open-air festival
All day Saturday
Starts 10:00 A.M.

Chagall Art Exhibition
Museum of Modern Art
Tue–Sun 9:00 A.M. to 5:00 P.M.
until 8:00 P.M. on Fridays

Jazz Concert
Lenny Duke, Jazz guitar
Blue Note Club
8:30 P.M. Friday

Friday 7:00 P.M.
Meet at train station

Part 2 When you have planned your weekend, discuss your schedule with another pair of students. How are they different?

Now Try This

Imagine that you have a change of plan. You forgot that your class will finish late on Friday and you will not be able to arrive until 10:00 P.M. Call your friend and rearrange your schedule.

(Student B looks at this page. Student A looks at page 61.)

Part 1 You are a sales representative for Sam's clothing catalog company. Read the catalog to see which items are on sale or not in stock.

Part 2 A customer will call you with his or her order. Persuade the customer to buy as many items as possible. Write down the customer's order.

Sam's Outdoor Clothing

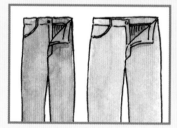  

Pure wool or cotton / polyester pants, wide or narrow styles

Colors: blue, brown, gray, black
Sizes: s, m, l
Price: $49.00
Customer's order: _____

Four-season nylon / down mix ski jackets, long or short styles

Colors: green, purple (purple not in stock), yellow ($20 off yellow)
Sizes: S–XL
Price: $229
Customer's order: _____

Hiking socks, 100% wool or cotton

Colors: white, gray, brown
Sizes: one size
Price: $8.50 (buy two pairs, get one pair free)
Customer's order: _____

Part 3 You are planning a trip to Thailand this winter and you need to buy T-shirts, a backpack, and sandals. Your favorite color is blue. Your clothing size is small. Your shoe size is 6. Read the information from Eddy's clothing catalog and decide which items you want to buy. Write down the items you will buy. Call the clothing catalog company and order the items you need. How much did you spend?

EDDY'S OUTDOOR CLOTHING

Genuine leather or nylon backpacks, waterproof, lightweight

Colors:

_____

Sizes: _____
Price: _____
Your order:

_____

Leather hiking sandals, high- or low-heel styles

Colors:

_____

Sizes:

_____

Price:

_____

Your order:

_____

Comfortable round-neck T-shirts, 100% cotton

Colors: _____

Sizes: _____

Price: _____

Your order:

_____

Now Try This

One of the items you bought in Part 3 has a problem. Call the company, explain what is wrong, and ask for a refund or an exchange.

(Student B looks at this page. Student A looks at page 69.)

Part 1 Read the information on the menu. Check the pronunciation of any difficult words with your teacher.

Part 2 You are the server. Answer the questions from your customer and take their order. Offer additional suggestions for desserts, drinks, or side dishes.

Menu

Appetizer

Soup of the Day (Today's soup of the day is fresh tomato and basil)

Avocado Florentine (Fresh avocado filled with shrimp)

Dessert

Flan (A creamy dessert made from eggs and milk)

Fresh Fruit Salad (Today's fresh fruits are: apple, melon, and pineapple.)

Main Course

Roast Lamb and Vegetable Kebabs. (Kebabs are small pieces of meat and vegetable (onions, peppers, and mushrooms) grilled on a stick. Served with rice or potatoes.)

Seafood Paella with Spicy Salsa (Paella is a mixture of rice, seafood, and vegetables. Salsa is a spicy sauce made from tomatoes and peppers. Served with green salad and Italian or Blue Cheese dressing.)

Beverages

Tea (hot or iced)
Coffee (espresso or cappuccino)
Herbal Tea (chamomile or orange spice)

Part 3 Now you are the customer. Put a check (✓) next to the dishes you want to order. Underline the dishes you need more information about. Go to the restaurant and order your meal. Ask questions about the items you don't understand.

Menu

Appetizer

Seafood Cocktail

Mushroom Quiche

Dessert

Cake

Ice Cream

Main Course

Chicken Chow Mein

Vegetable Lasagna

Beverages

Tea, Coffee, Herbal Tea

Now Try This

With a partner, write your own menu. Find a new partner and role-play a conversation between server and customer.

(Student B looks at this page. Student A looks at page 77.)

Part 1 You are an airline representative at Honolulu International Airport in Hawaii. A customer has just arrived and is going to make a complaint about lost luggage. Think of three possible solutions to the problem. Write down your ideas here.

LOST LUGGAGE

1. _____

2. _____

3. _____

Part 2 Your partner is making a complaint. Ask about the problem, and suggest two or three different solutions. Try to find the best solution, but if it is impossible, apologize. Remember the following information:

• Your company will offer some money only if the suitcase is not found within seven days.

• Your company does not deliver lost luggage to the hotel.

• Passengers usually have travel insurance for this kind of problem.

Part 3 After talking to your manager, you find out that the luggage will be on the next plane, which will arrive in about six hours. Ask the passenger to wait in the airport or come back in six hours. Find a successful solution to the problem. Remember the following information:

• You can offer coupons for free meals and drinks in the airport cafe.

• You can pay for cab fare to the hotel and back to the airport.

• You can offer a free return ticket if the suitcase is not found.

Now Try This

Finally, the passenger leaves for the hotel with the suitcase. Tell your partner about your experience.

(Student B looks at this page. Student A looks at page 95.)

Part 1 Read the information about Honolulu and Bangkok. Make a list of adjectives you could use to compare these two cities.

_____   _____   _____

_____   _____   _____

Part 2 Compare the cities using the adjectives in your list. Tell your partner which city you think is more interesting to visit and why. Your partner also has some information about two different cities.
Ask questions and find out which city is more interesting to visit and why?

Part 3 Fill out the chart for all four cities.

Best...	Food	Sight-seeing	Nightlife	Shopping
Honolulu				
Bangkok				

Now Try This

Imagine you are planning a trip around the world with your friend. You can visit four cities anywhere in the world. Which cities would you visit and why? Tell the class about your plan.

Audio script

Unit 1

GIVE IT A TRY   PAGE 3

1. Introducing yourself
A: Hello. My name's Patricia.
B: Hi. I'm Bo-wei.

2. Getting the name right
A: Hello. My name's Patricia.
B: Sorry, what's your name again?
A: Patricia, but please call me Pat.

3. Asking someone's occupation
A: What do you do?
B: I'm a computer programmer.
A: Oh, are you? That's great!
B: Yeah. How about you?
A: I'm studying medicine.

4. Asking for more information
A: What do you do?
B: I'm a student.
A: Really? What school do you go to?
B: I go to Boston College.
A: What are you studying?
B: Computer science and English.

LISTEN TO THIS   PAGE 4

1
B: Great wedding, isn't it? Are you a friend of Mike's or of Susan's?
J: Susan. We went to college together.
B: Really? I work with Mike. Oh, by the way, my name's Bob. Bob Bradley.
J: Hi, Bob. I'm June. June Owens.
B: I'm sorry. I didn't get your first name.
J: It's June. Nice to meet you.
B: You, too. So, what do you do, June?
J: I'm a chef. How about you?
B: I'm a computer programmer.

2
J: Tim always has great parties, doesn't he?
K: Yeah. Do you go to school with Tim?
J: Yeah. We study art together at Columbia. How about you?
K: I'm studying fashion design at City College. My name's Kim Lee, by the way.
J: Nice to meet you, Kim. I'm John Hunt.
K: Well, John, would you like to dance?
J: I'd love to.

3
T: What did you think of that film?
M: It was fascinating! I learned a lot about life in Paris.
T: Have you been to this film festival before?
M: No. It's my first time. It's nice to meet you. I'm Mario Pirelli. Please call me Mario.
T: OK, Mario. My name's Tomomi Sato.
M: I'm sorry, I didn't catch your first name.

T: It's Tomomi. What do you do, Mario?
M: I'm a journalist. I work for CNO Radio. How about you?
T: I'm a music major at NYU.

GIVE IT A TRY   PAGE 7

1. Names
A: Could I have your name, please?
B: It's Bo-wei. Bo-wei Zhang.
A: How do you spell your first name?
B: It's B-o dash w-e-i.

2. Addresses
A: Where do you live?
B: I live at 2418 Graystone Road.
A: Is that in New York?
B: Yes, that's right.

3. Telephone and e-mail
A: What's your telephone number?
B: It's 917-555-9758.
A: And please give me your e-mail address.
B: It's bowei33@internet.com.
A: Thank you.

LISTEN TO THIS   PAGE 8

J: Hi. I'd like to apply for a credit card.
S: All right. Please have a seat. Now, are you a regular customer at Lacy's?
J: Oh, yes. I love this store.
S: Good. Could I have your name, please?
J: Jean Sands.
S: How do you spell your first name?
J: It's J-e-a-n. Oh, and my last name is S-a-n-d-s.
S: Thank you. And where do you live?
J: 30 Jackson Street.
S: I'm sorry. Did you say 30 or 13?
J: Thirty. Three zero.
S: Is that in Boston?
J: No, it's in Salem. The zip code is 07310.
S: And what's your occupation?
J: I'm a chef at the Bayside Hotel.
S: Chef at the Bayside Hotel? All right. I also need your telephone number.
J: My home number is 617-654-1315. My work number is 617-783-9471.
S: Do you have an e-mail address?
J: Yes, it's jsands@email.com.
S: OK. I think that's everything. You'll receive your card in about two weeks.
J: Thank you very much.

Unit 2

GIVE IT A TRY   PAGE 11

1. Describing your family
A: Do you have any brothers or sisters?
B: No, I'm an only child.

2. Marital status and children
A: Is your brother married?
B: Yes, he is.
A: Does he have any children?
B: Yes, he has two children.

3. Talking about age
A: How old is your sister?
B: She's 24.

LISTEN TO THIS   PAGE 12

1
This is me with my two brothers. I'm the youngest. Dan is four years older than John. And John is a year older than me. I'm trying to blow out the candles on the cake and they're both laughing at me.

2
My grandmother gave me a really beautiful silver necklace as a 21st birthday gift. It used to belong to her mother. Here I am wearing the necklace and standing next to my mother and my grandmother. Don't we all look alike?

3
This is me dancing with my father, and there's my aunt Ida and uncle Ted dancing together, too. Ted is my father's younger brother, but they look the same age.

4
And these are my two nieces, Sarah and Pauleen. Don't they look cute in their party dresses? Those are my brother Dan's children. Sarah is five and Pauleen is a year younger. I don't think they knew what the party was for, but they had a great time!

LISTEN TO THIS   PAGE 16

D: OK. So everyone here actually saw the man who drove his motorcycle through the flower garden at City Hall?
All: Yes! I did! I saw him!
D: Quiet, please. I can't listen to everyone talking at the same time. I'll speak to each of you alone in my office.

1
D: What did he look like?
W1: Well, let me see. I think he was short and very thin.
D: And what was his hair like?
W1: He had, um, light brown hair. It was medium length and curly.
D: Age?
W1: I guess…early 30s.
D: So, he was between 31 and 33 years old?
W1: Yes, that's right.
D: One more question. Do you remember what he was wearing?
W1: He had on a blue and red soccer shirt, jeans, and red sneakers.

D: Well, thank you for coming in.
W1: You're welcome.

2

D: First of all, thank you for waiting.
W2: Oh, no problem. I like to help the police when I can.
D: Fine. Now, what did the man look like?
W2: He was pretty tall and thin. I think he was about 20.
D: Good. Now, his hair. What was it like?
W2: Oh. It was wavy and kind of short. It was blond or brown. Wait, it was blond.
D: And what about his clothes?
W2: Tsk. Terrible. Not fashionable at all.
D: I mean, what did he have on?
W2: Well, he was wearing a blue polo shirt with red stripes and a pair of brown pants. Can you believe it? And black shoes. Blue, brown, and black? Terrible.
D: OK. That's everything. Thanks again, and could you send in the next person, please?

3

D: Come in, please, and have a seat. So, can you describe the man for me?
M: Sure. What do you want to know?
D: Let's start with the clothes. What was he wearing?
M: Hmmm…. I think it was a blue shirt.
D: Anything else?
M: Maybe black pants.
D: How about height? How tall was he?
M: I'm pretty sure he was tall, but he was sitting down. I remember he was pretty thin. And his hair…his hair was brown and curly. It was about shoulder length.
D: Just one more question. His age. About how old was he?
M: I guess he was a teenager. In his late teens. He looked kind of young.
D: OK. Thank you for the information. I'm sure we'll catch him soon.

Unit 3

GIVE IT A TRY   PAGE 19

1. Asking where things are (informal)

A: Where is the copy paper?
B: It's on the shelf.

2. Asking where things are (formal)

A: Do you know where my computer disks are?
B: They're on the top shelf between the printer and the paper.

LISTEN TO THIS   PAGE 20

1

A: Hey, Margo! Do you know where the scissors are?
B: Aren't they in the desk drawer?
A: No. That's the first place I looked.
B: Oh, I know. I was using them in the kitchen. Try next to the telephone.
A: Oh, yeah. I've got them. Thanks.

2

A: What are you looking for?
B: My book. I can't find my book.
A: I saw it on the coffee table this morning.
B: Here it is. It was under the newspaper.

3

A: Excuse me. Do you sell computer disks?
B: Oh, yes. We sell all types of disks.
A: Great. And where do you keep them?
B: Do you see the computer section?
A: Over there next to the video tapes?
B: No, on the other side. That's right. They're on the middle shelf between the paper and the computer games.
A: I found them! Thanks for your help.

4

A: Where did I put my eyeglasses? Mark, have you seen them?
B: Are they on the top shelf of the bookcase?
A: No, I already looked there.
B: Maybe they fell down under the desk?
A: I hope not! They're my only pair! Oh, here they are, behind the calendar. Now why did I put them there?

GIVE IT A TRY   PAGE 23

1. Describing things

A: There is a big, round, red ball. There is a small, blue, triangular thing in front of the ball.
A: It's number 1.

LISTEN TO THIS   PAGE 24

1

My invention is flat and round and has a very small hole right in the middle of it. It's quite small. You put it in a special machine and you can listen to music on it or you can store information on it.

2

My invention is something you can't touch. You get to it through your computer. It's used for communicating with other people, even people thousands of miles away. It's used for sending and storing information.

3

My invention is made of metal and plastic. It comes in lots of colors. It makes musical noises. It's very useful if you are on a train or in a store and you need to talk to someone far away. It's also used for taking messages.

4

My invention is small and box-shaped. It's usually made of metal, but sometimes metal and plastic. It uses electricity. It gets very hot and if you touch it you'll get burned. You usually find one in the kitchen. It's often used at breakfast time. You put bread in it.

5

My invention is made of plastic. It comes in many colors. It's small and rectangular. It's very thin, almost as thin as paper! It has a magnetic strip with coded data on it. It's used in stores and in bank machines. It helps you spend your money.

6

These are very, very small and round. They are made of plastic and they are transparent. People can use them anywhere—outside, at home, when they are playing sports or swimming. They're used to help you see better.

Review Unit 1

LISTEN TO THIS   PAGE 26

BM: Yes, how can I help you?
M: I'd like to open a savings account.
BM: Certainly. We'll have to fill out a few forms. Could I have your name, please?
M: My name is Meena Patel.
BM: Could you spell that for me, please?
M: My first name is Meena, M-e-e-n-a. My last name is Patel, P-a-t-e-l.
BM: Thank you. Is it Mrs. or Ms.?
M: Ms.
BM: Fine. And could I have your address?
M: 301 Victoria Avenue, Long Beach, California.
BM: And what's the zip code?
M: 90747.
BM: Could I have your telephone number?
M: 310-555-8268.
BM: And what do you do?
M: I'm a fashion designer. I work for Silk Designs.
BM: Do you have an e-mail address?
M: It's mpatel@silkdesigns.com.
BM: That's fine. Now I just need an ID card and we're all set.

Review Unit 2

LISTEN TO THIS   PAGE 26

Look! Stephanie just sent me photos from her wedding. Doesn't she look gorgeous? She chose a white silk dress for the wedding. It really looks perfect. And look, she's holding white roses, too. Henry looks great, too. He looks so slim in that beautiful gray suit. Henry's father is quite tall. His name's Dan—he's the one in the gray suit with gray hair. That's Bob—Henry's brother—he's very handsome in the light blue shirt. And over here, that's Henry's mother, Gemma—the short woman with blond hair. Those are Henry's nieces. One is about 13. Her name's Eileen. The other one is only 8 years old—she looks so cute in her blue and white dress with the flowers in her hair. Her name's Gina. And that's Justin, Henry's cousin. He said I looked beautiful in my blue dress. What do you think?

Review Unit 3

LISTEN TO THIS   PAGE 27

1. It's in the middle of the floor.
2. They're on the middle shelf, next to the dictionary.
3. It's on the bottom shelf.
4. It's in the corner next to the window.

5. It's under the desk.
6. It's made of metal and glass. It's round. It's used for telling the time.
7. It's made of paper. It's square and quite thick. It's used for finding words.
8. It's on the desk next to the computer.
9. It's made of paper. It's square and thin. It's used for planning your time.
10. It's made of metal and plastic and glass. It's shaped like a cube. It's used for storing information, writing letters, going on the Internet…

Unit 4

GIVE IT A TRY   PAGE 29

1. Days and dates
A: When's your birthday?
B: It's on October 24.

2. Starting and finishing times
A: What time does the movie *Hollywood* start?
B: It starts at 6:45.
A: And what time does it end?
B: It ends around 8:30.

LISTEN TO THIS   PAGE 30

1
A: City Park swimming pool. Good morning.
B: Good morning. Could you tell me if the pool is open today?
A: Yes. The pool opens at 10:00.
B: Oh, good. And what time does it close?
A: We have our summer hours now, so we close at 10:00 P. M.
B: OK. Thank you very much.
A: You're welcome.

2
Hello. Thank you for calling the Golden Cinema Theater. Our specialty is movies from the good old days. Tonight we have two movies. The first is *Casablanca*, with Humphrey Bogart and Ingrid Bergman. It starts at 7:15 and ends at 9:00. Our second feature is *Roman Holiday*, starring Gregory Peck and Audrey Hepburn. It starts at 9:30 and ends at 11:30. The admission price is $7.50. Doors open at 6:45.

3
A: City Stadium. Can I help you?
B: Yes. Do you have any more tickets for the concert on Friday night?
A: Do you mean the rock concert? Yes, we still have some $25 tickets left.
B: Great. And is the box office open now?
A: Yes. We're open from 10:00 to 8:00.
B: Oh, by the way, when does the show start?
A: It starts at 8:00.
B: And what time does it end?
A: Well, probably around midnight.
B: Thanks a lot.
A: No problem.

GIVE IT A TRY   PAGE 33

1. Describing locations
A: Excuse me. Do you know where the post office is?
B: Sure. It's on Elm Street, across from the hardware store.

2. Giving directions
PRACTICE 1
A: Excuse me. Which way is the camera store?
B: It's down 20th street on the right.

PRACTICE 2
A: Where can I go to get some cash?
B: You need to go to the bank. It's down this street on the left, just past the bakery.

LISTEN TO THIS   PAGE 34

1
A: It's a short walk from here. It's on Fourth Avenue, just past the post office.
B: So I walk up this street?
A: That's right. It's at the end of the third block, on the corner, across from the Grand Hotel.
B: I've got it. Thanks.
A: No problem.

2
A: Just walk up Fourth one block to 20th Street. Turn left and walk one block to Third Avenue. Go up two more blocks, and you'll see it on the left, across from the music store.
B: Let me see…. Up Fourth to 20th, left on 20th to Third, up Third about two blocks. It's on the left side of the street?
A: That's it.
B: Great. Thanks for your help.

3
A: Go up this street and take the second right—that's at 21st Street. Stay on the right side of the street. It's in the middle of that block, between the hardware store and the men's clothing store.
B: OK, so I want the second right, and it's in the middle of that block between what and what?
A: Between the hardware store—I think it's called Mel's—and a men's clothing store. You can't miss it.
B: I'm sure I'll find it. Thanks a lot.
A: Sure.

4
A: Sorry, we're not from around here.
B: Well, thanks anyway.
C: Wait! I saw it when we came out of the hotel. Do you know the Good Sports Grill?
B: No, I don't.
C: It's easy. You walk up this street three blocks and turn right. Walk over one more block. You'll be at the corner of Fifth and 22nd. You'll see it on Fifth Avenue, on the other corner across the street from the Good Sports Grill.

B: So, I have to get to the corner of Fifth and 22nd, and it'll be on my right?
C: Uh-huh. Across from the restaurant.
B: Thank you.
C: My pleasure.

Unit 5

LISTEN TO THIS   PAGE 38
L: Thanks for coming out with me tonight.
A: Thanks for asking.
L: So. Dinner first. We could go out to a nice Chinese restaurant. I love the food at the Golden Dragon.
A: Oh, Lee. I don't really like Chinese food. I really just want a burger and fries.
L: Oh, I see. I guess a hamburger and french fries will be all right tonight.
A: What do you want to do after dinner? There's a new science-fiction movie at the Star Cinema. I really love science-fiction movies.
L: Sorry, Alissa. I hate science fiction. But, you know…I want to see the new documentary at the Triplex theater. Do you like documentaries?
A: No, they usually put me to sleep. I can't stand them. Hmm. Well, I have one more idea. We can go bowling. I like to bowl.
L: That's a good idea. I like bowling, too.

GIVE IT A TRY   PAGE 41

1. Agreeing and disagreeing with likes and dislikes
A: I hate animated movies.
B: Really? I don't. I think they're fantastic.

LISTEN TO THIS   PAGE 42

1
A: Do you know why I love Sundays?
B: Sure, you don't work today.
A: That's true, but also, there are sports on TV all day.
B: Oh. Yeah.
A: I love football, but I can't stand golf! So what do you want to watch? Football? Basketball? Which one do you like?
B: To be honest, I don't really like watching sports. Maybe I'll read.

2
A: Do you know any good places for dinner around here?
B: Well, I really like Cafe Pronto. They have fantastic Italian food.
A: I love Cafe Pronto! I haven't been there in a long time. I can't remember, though, is it very expensive?
B: That's another good thing about it. It's not expensive at all.
A: Sounds perfect. Ler's go.

3
A: This book is just excellent. I'm really enjoying it.

B: What is it?
A: *Lord of the Rings*. Have you read it?
B: No, but I saw the movie.
A: Do you want to read it when I'm done?
B: No, thanks. I love reading books, but not when I already know the story.
A: Really? It doesn't bother me.

4
A: What's up?
B: I have a terrible headache. You know I went shopping for clothes today.
A: That gave you a headache?
B: I went into one of those stores that sells mostly jeans, and they were playing really loud music.
A: I know what you mean. I can't stand that.
B: Neither can I! Where's the aspirin?

Unit 6

GIVE IT A TRY   PAGE 45

1. Accepting invitations
A: Do you feel like going out for dinner Saturday?
B: Sure. I'd love to.

3. Getting more information
A: Would you like to come to a party this Saturday?
B: Sounds good! Where is it?
A: It's at my place.
B: What time does it start?
A: It's at one o'clock.
B: Who's going?
A: Some people from school.
B: OK! I'll see you there.

LISTEN TO THIS   PAGE 47

1
M: Here it is, Friday night. Do you want to go dancing?
Y: Well, not really. I'm kind of tired. I had a pretty hard week. But how about going out to listen to some music?
M: What kind of music?
Y: How about a little jazz?
M: Yeah. That sounds nice.
Y: What about the Club Blue Note?
M: I've never heard of it.
Y: My sister was there last week. She said the food and the music are terrific.
M: Really? What kind of food do they serve?
Y: Mostly sandwiches and salads.
M: Is it expensive?
Y: She said the prices are very good. So, do you feel like trying it?
M: Why not? I'll just get my coat.

2
O: Hi, Ben. What's up?
B: What about coming over on Sunday afternoon for a baseball party?
O: A baseball party? What's that?
B: This Sunday's game is pretty important, so I'm inviting a bunch of people from our class over to my place to watch it.

O: Who's coming?
B: So far, there's Han, Yuki, Stefan, Anna Maria, Ricardo, Lise, and Yong.
O: I'd love to, but I can't. My brother is coming back from Mexico City. I have to pick him up at the airport.
B: That's too bad. Well, how about coming over after you get back from the airport?
O: That's a good idea. Can I bring anything?
B: Whatever you like to drink. We'll order pizza for dinner.

GIVE IT A TRY   PAGE 49

1. Suggesting another day
A: How about going out for coffee after the show?
B: I'm really sorry. I can't make it.
A: Oh, that's too bad. Well, how about Friday then?
B: Great! That sounds good.

2. Setting the time and the place
A: How about going to see the Rocket Dogs at the Garage Club on Thursday?
B: Sure. Where do you want to meet?
A: How about meeting in front of the club?
B: Great. What time?
A: Why don't we meet at 7:15?
B: Fine. See you at 7:15.
A: OK. See you!

3. Changing plans
A: How about going shopping on Saturday?
B: OK. Where do you want to meet?
A: Let's meet outside the station at one.
B: Could we meet outside the department store instead?
A: OK. But could we meet a little later, at 1:30?
B: Sure. No problem.

4. Adding to plans
A: How about going swimming tomorrow?
B: That sounds good. Do you want to have lunch afterward?
A: Good idea! Let's meet outside the swimming pool at 10:00.
B: Sounds good. See you then.

LISTEN TO THIS   PAGE 50

L: Hi, Sandy. What's happening tonight?
S: Do you feel like playing tennis?
L: I haven't played tennis in ages. How about squash? I'm better at squash!
S: Sounds good. Is 7:00 all right?
L: Could we make it a little later? I have a class until 6:30.
S: That's no problem. What time do you want to meet?
L: I can meet at 7:30, but how about having dinner first? I didn't have time for lunch today.
S: OK. I know a cool Mexican restaurant.
L: I don't really like Mexican food. Could we go to a Chinese restaurant instead?
S: Yeah, the Hong Kong Garden is really close to the courts.

L: I've eaten there before and I liked it.
S: Then let's meet at the restaurant!
L: Good idea. Maybe we could get a drink at the Mexican place after our game?
S: OK! See you at the restaurant at 7:30 then.
L: Great! I'll try not to be late.

Review Unit 4

LISTEN TO THIS   PAGE 52

Thank you for calling the Star Cinema. The following show times are good through Thursday, May 14. Star Cinema is proud to present *Galactica*, the exciting new science-fiction adventure with spectacular special effects. Showing evenings at 7:00 and 9:20, with Saturday and Sunday matinees at noon and 3:15. Show time two hours and ten minutes. Also showing is the animated horror, *Mask of the Mummy*. Showing daily at noon and at 3:20. Suitable for children 12 and over. Show time one hour and 40 minutes. Don't miss the suspense thriller *Broken Window*, winner of the Top Film Award for Mystery and Suspense, showing Saturdays and Sundays at 5:10 and 6:45. Show time one hour and 55 minutes. For ticket prices and reservations, press 1 now, or stay on the line.

Review Unit 5

LISTEN TO THIS   PAGE 52

B: Hey, Mike, what are you doing this weekend?
M: The weather's supposed to be warm this weekend. Perfect for jogging!
B: Oh, yeah? What time are you going?
M: About six.
B: Six! That's way too early for me. I hate getting up early. Especially on Saturdays. I prefer to go to the pool.
M: The pool? Why do you like to be indoors when the weather's warm?
B: But swimming is really good for you. I like it better than jogging.
M: Oh, yeah? Why?
B: Well it's less stress on your knees and joints, and it's more relaxing.
M: I guess so, but it's a great feeling to run in the fresh air.
B: How about meeting up for dinner on Saturday evening?
M: Sure, what time?
B: About 8:00 P. M.?
M: Eight! That's way too late for my dinner. I have to be in bed by ten.
B: So you can get up early, right?

Review Unit 6

LISTEN TO THIS   PAGE 53

C: Maria, do you want to go to my roomate's birthday party this weekend?
M: Sure, I'd love to! When is it?

C: It's on Saturday night.
M: Sounds good. What should I bring?
C: Just whatever you like to drink.
M: How about a birthday gift?
C: No, the girls at the dorm got together and bought her a gift. Don't worry.
M: What time will it start?
C: 8:00. Do you want to go out to eat first?
M: OK, but I have a class until 6:30. How about meeting at Tom's Grill at 6:45?
C: Sounds perfect. They have great pizza. We'll go to my dorm for the party after.
M: By the way, there's a Latin American film festival at the Cinema Club on Sunday. Do you want to go?
C: What's playing there?
M: Well, there's a film about Patagonia that sounds really interesting. It's on at 2:30.
C: Patagonia? I'm not sure. Let me think about it. I'll tell you on Saturday, OK?
M: OK.

Unit 7

| GIVE IT A TRY | PAGE 55 |

1. Getting and giving help

PRACTICE 1
A: Excuse me. Could you help me?
B: Certainly. What can I help you with?
A: I'm looking for men's shirts.

PRACTICE 2
A: Can I help you?
B: Yes, please. I'm looking for men's shirts.

2. Getting information
A: Excuse me. Could you help me?
B: Certainly. What can I help you with?
A: Do you have this sweater in black?
B: Yes, we do.

3. Asking prices
A: Excuse me. How much is this jacket?
B: It's $249.
A: Is it on sale?
B: Yes, it's $10.00 off.
A: Great. I'll take it.
B: Will that be cash or credit?
A: Cash.

| LISTEN TO THIS | PAGE 56 |

1
S: Excuse me. Could you help me?
S1: Certainly. What can I do for you?
S: We're looking for a girl's T-shirt. I really like this style. Do you have it in small?
S1: Let me see. Medium, large, extra large…. Here we are. Small.
S: Oh, I don't really want yellow. What other colors do you have?
S1: It comes in red, pink, and light blue.
S: The pink one is nice. How much is it?
S1: It's $18. But if you buy one, you get the second one half price.
S: Oh, I only need one. It's for my sister's birthday.

2
S2: Good afternoon. Is there something I can help you with?
Y: Yes, we'd like to see some men's gloves.
S2: Yes, sir. Do you know what color or size you'd like?
Y: What sizes do you have?
S2: We have most styles in stock, in small, medium, and large.
Y: I think my father takes medium. This style is perfect. Do you have them in tan?
S2: I'm sorry, sir. These only come in black and brown.
Y: Hmm. And how much are they?
S2: They're usually $50, but they're on sale this week. Half price.
Y: In that case, I think I'll take brown.

3
S3: Hi, can I help you with something?
S: Yes, please. I'm interested in a handbag for my mother.
S3: Of course. This red one is very nice. It also comes in white and in navy. The quality is excellent and it's only $150.
S: That's quite expensive. Do you have a cheaper one?
S3: I'm sorry, this is the only style we have.
S: That's too bad. Well, thanks anyway.

| GIVE IT A TRY | PAGE 59 |

1. Comparing things (1)
A: Which hat do you like better?
B: I like the gray hat better than the blue one.

2. Comparing things (2)
A: Which boots do you like better?
B: I like the black ones better than the brown ones.
A: Why?
B: Because they're more stylish.

3. Returning things
A: I'd like to exchange these shoes.
B: What's wrong with them?
A: I don't really like them.
B: Of course, we can exchange them.

| LISTEN TO THIS | PAGE 60 |

1
S: Yes. What can I do for you today?
C: I'd like to return this coat and get a refund, please.
A: I see. And what is the reason?
C: I'll show you. It's too small.
A: Oh, yes. I see. Do you have your receipt?
C: Here it is.

2
C: Pardon me. Could you help me?
S: Sure. What can I do for you?
C: Well, I'd like to exchange this CD.
S: What's wrong with it?
C: My brother gave it to me for my birthday. It's his favorite music, but I want something quieter.

S: I'm really sorry, but there are no exchanges on CDs once they've been opened.

3
S: Good morning, sir. How can I help you today?
C: I'd like to exchange this sweater, please. I just bought it about half an hour ago. I have the receipt right here in my bag.
S: What's the problem?
C: I decided that I don't really like the color. I think I like the orange one better.
S: Yes, the orange one is a nice color, isn't it? Much brighter than the brown one. Just a moment, I'll switch them for you.

Unit 8

| GIVE IT A TRY | PAGE 63 |

1. Discussing the menu
A: What are you going to have, Akemi?
B: I'll have pancakes and a cup of tea.

2. Ordering
A: What would you like?
B: I think I'll have scrambled eggs. With toast, please.

3. Adding extra information
A: Excuse me.
B: Good afternoon. What would you like?
A: I'd like the hot roast beef sandwich.
B: Yes, sir. Would you like soup or salad with that?
A: I'd like a salad, please.
B: What kind of dressing would you like?
A: French, please.
B: And what kind of dessert would you like?
A: Vanilla ice cream, please.

| LISTEN TO THIS | PAGE 65 |

S: Hi. Is everybody ready to order?
W: Yes, I think so. Anne? What are you going to have? They say the pasta is really good here.
A: Pasta sounds good, but I think I'd like a mushroom pizza, with a green salad and iced tea.
S: What kind of dressing do you want on the salad?
A: Italian, please.
W: Lisa, how about you?
L: I'm not sure yet. Dave, you go ahead.
D: OK. I'll have the turkey sandwich with a large order of french fries, and a coffee. What about you, Wen?
W: And I'll have the seafood pasta, with iced tea, please. Oh, and a green salad with thousand island dressing.
L: I think I'll try the pasta, too. I love seafood. No salad for me.
S: And what would you like to drink?
L: Oh, just water, please.
W: I think that's all, or do you want to order dessert now? Lisa says they have excellent pies and cakes here.

L: Yes, the cakes look really good. I saw them when we came in.
A: I prefer ice cream.
D: Me, too.
W: I think we'll wait until later with our dessert. Thank you.

1. Describing food
A: Could you tell me what gazpacho is?
B: It's a spicy soup served cold. It's made from tomatoes and vegetables.

2. Offering additional food or drink
A: Would you like something to drink?
B: Do you have any iced tea?
A: I'm sorry we don't. We have lemonade or soda.
B: I'll have lemonade, then.

3. Offering other suggestions
A: Would you like anything else?
B: Yes, could you bring me some more rolls?
A: Certainly.

1
S: Would you like something to drink?
W: Do you have apple juice?
S: We have orange, tomato, and cranberry.
W: OK, I'll take orange. A large, please.

2
M: I'd like to order dessert.
S: Yes, what would you like?
M: What kind of pie do you have?
S: Pecan, peach, and apple.
M: Is it homemade?
S: Of course!
M: Could I have pecan pie with vanilla ice cream on the side?
S: Certainly.

3
W: I'd like a small ice cream, please.
S: What kind of ice cream would you like?
W: Do you have cherry?
S: No, I'm afraid we've run out. The closest we have is strawberry.
W: I don't like strawberry.
S: We have chocolate, vanilla, or how about mango? That's our newest flavor. It's very popular.
W: OK, I'll try the mango.

Unit 9

1. Making small requests
A: Excuse me. Could I borrow a pencil, please?
B: Sure. Here you are.

2. Making larger requests
A: Do you think I could borrow your laptop for a few hours?
B: I'm sorry. I need it right now.

A: But my computer isn't working and I have to write a report.
B: OK. You can have it after I'm done.

3. Asking for favors
PRACTICE 1
A: Would you please open the door for me?
B: Sure. No problem.

PRACTICE 2
A: Would you please open the door for me?
B: I'm sorry, my hands are full!

1
W: Oh, no! What happened to all my coins?
M: Don't worry. I have lots of change.
W: Do you have three quarters?
M: Sure. Here you go.

2
W: OK…books, tape player, tapes, purse…let's see…yeah…that's everything.
B: Can I carry something for you?
W: No. That's OK. I've got it all. But could you please get the door and the lights for me?
B: Of course!

3
B: Oh, wow. I'm exhausted.
S: Why?
B: I stayed up until 3:00 A. M. studying for that test today. Sally, could you do the dishes today? I know it's my turn, but I'm just too tired.
S: No, I can't help you. You always have some excuse for not doing your chores. I cleaned the house and made dinner, so you have to do the dishes. Now!
B: OK…I'll do them.

4
W: Have you seen the rain? It's pouring out there!
M: No, really? I have to walk to the bank on my lunch break.
W: Did you remember your umbrella this morning?
M: No, I forgot it. If you're not going outside at lunch, could I please borrow yours?
W: I'm sorry. I didn't bring mine today either.

5
M: Hi, Alison. How're you?
A: Great, Marge. What's new? Would you like to come in for coffee?
M: I'd love to. But to tell you the truth, I'm right in the middle of making a cake, and I'm out of sugar. Do you think I could borrow some?
A: Oh, sure. No problem. How much do you need?
M: Just half a cup.
A: Wait a minute. I'll get it for you.

6
W: Oh…there they are. Of course they're on the top shelf. It's no use. Aagh! Oh, excuse me!

S: Yes, ma'am. What can I do for you?
W: Hi. Sorry to bother you. Could you do me a favor? I need one of those jars of pickles on the top shelf, but I can't reach it. Could you please get it down for me?
S: Sure. Here you go.

1. Complaining politely
A: Excuse me. I have a problem with my room.
B: What's the problem?
A: I asked for a non-smoking room, but I got a smoking room.

2. Requesting action or change
A: Could you change my room, please?
B: I'm sorry. We can't now, but we can change your room tomorrow.
A: Thanks for your help.

1
A: Excuse me!
B: Yes, ma'am. What can I do for you?
A: I have a problem with this coffeemaker, and I want my money back.
B: Well, what seems to be the problem?
A: The problem is that it doesn't work! I've only used it three times.
B: I'd be happy to exchange it for you.
A: Thank you, but I'd like a refund, please. I invited six people to my place for dinner last night. After dinner, I plugged in the coffeemaker, I put in the coffee and water, I turned it on, and nothing happened! I was very embarrassed. No. I'd like my money back.
B: Of course. A refund is no problem at all. I'm sorry you've had so much trouble.
A: That's OK. And thank you for your help.

2
A: Next, please!
B: Yes, I just received my telephone bill, and there's a problem with it.
A: And what exactly is the problem?
B: There's a collect call from Finland on it, and I don't know anyone in Finland! I'm very upset. Could you please take the charge off my bill?
A: May I see your bill, please?
B: Certainly. Here it is. On July 1. I really don't know anybody in Finland.
A: OK. Don't worry. I'll take the call off. Let's see…. It was $42.00. Your bill was $66.10, minus $42.00, so your new total is $24.10. I'm very sorry about the mistake.
B: That's OK. It wasn't your fault.

Review Unit 7

J: This is a really good store. I bet you can find everything you need for your trip right here.

K: I hope so. I have a lot to do before I leave.

J: Do you know what you need?

K: Not too much, really. Pants, a jacket, and a sweater.

J: Here are the pants. Oh! This is a nice pair. They're black, so they'll go with everything.

K: Except, if it's sunny, they'll be too hot. Besides, I already have black ones at home. How about these pink pants?

J: They're a much nicer color.

K: And they feel like better quality, too. I'll try them on later. Let's look for a sweater now…. I like this purple one.

J: Do you? I really think it's too plain. What do you think of this white one? It's fancier, so you could wear it in the evening.

K: I know, but the purple one is looser. It'll be more comfortable. Anyway I have some fancy sweaters at home.

J: Well, try the purple then.

K: Let's see, I guess the last thing is the jacket.

J: Look at this beige suede jacket. It's beautiful, but I know it's too heavy for summer.

K: It's also too expensive! I don't want to spend that much money. Do you see any cotton jackets?

J: Over here. Oh, these are much lighter.

K: And the price is more reasonable, too.

Review Unit 8

LISTEN TO THIS   **PAGES 78**

S: Have you decided yet?

M: Yes, I think so. Marian?

W: Yes, I'll have the salmon teriyaki, please.

S: And what kind of potatoes would you like with that?

W: Baked, please. For the vegetable, I'd like broccoli.

S: And would you care for soup or salad to start?

M: What is your soup today?

S: We have cream of cauliflower and french onion.

W: Oh, they both sound heavy. I think I'll have a salad, please.

S: Very good. With what kind of dressing?

W: I'd like blue cheese. Oh wait, what is the Italian dressing made from?

S: It's oil and vinegar with Italian herbs.

W: I'll have Italian dressing, please.

S: Certainly. And you, sir, what will you have?

M: Those lobster tails sound good.

S: I'm very sorry, sir. We don't have any lobster left.

M: No lobster? Well…I guess I'll take the steak then. Could you tell the chef I like my steak very rare.

S: Of course. Mashed, boiled, or baked potatoes?

M: Mashed, please.

S: Vegetable?

M: I'd like asparagus.

S: And soup or salad?

M: I think I'm going to try the cream of cauliflower.

S: And would you care for any dessert?

W: We'll decide later, if that's all right. But could you bring me some extra butter with my potato?

S: Certainly. Anything to drink?

W: An iced coffee, please.

M: Make that two.

Review Unit 9

LISTEN TO THIS   **PAGES 79**

1

W: Excuse me. Could you help me, please? I'd like to return this blouse.

S: Do you have your receipt?

W: Yes, here it is.

S: What was the problem with the blouse?

W: I washed it once and it shrunk! Look! It was size 10, and now it's size 4!

S: We can offer you a store credit for the same amount, and you can buy any other clothing item in the store.

W: But I'd like a refund, please.

S: I'm afraid we don't usually give refunds.

W: OK, I guess I'll take the store credit then.

2

M: Excuse me. I'd like to return this watch, please.

S: What's the problem with it?

M: It's slow! Every day it gets about ten minutes slower!

S: Oh, dear! I think we'll have to send it back to the manufacturer. Would you like to choose another watch or get a refund?

M: I'd like a refund please.

S: Yes, of course. Do you have your receipt?

3

W: Excuse me. I'd like to return this camera.

S: Do you have a receipt?

W: Yes, here it is.

S: What was the problem with the camera?

W: The front of the camera won't open.

S: Would you like a replacement?

W: Thank you. Yes, please.

Unit 10

GIVE IT A TRY   **PAGE 81**

1. Giving and getting personal information (1)

A: Where are you from?

B: I'm from Canada, originally.

A: Were you born there?

B: Yes, I was born in Montreal.

2. Giving and getting personal information (2)

A: Did you go to school here?

B: No, I went to school in Boston.

A: Did you go to college right after high school?

B: Yes, I started college right away.

LISTEN TO THIS   **PAGE 83**

S: That's enough about me. How about you? Were you born in Los Angeles?

G: No, actually, I was born in Seattle, but I guess you could say I grew up all over the world.

S: Huh? What do you mean?

G: Well, my dad was in the air force, so we moved around a lot, starting when I was two. That was when we moved to Japan…just outside Tokyo.

S: Wow. Did you go to school there?

G: No, my father was sent to Germany after that. We moved to Munich in 1991, when I was five. I started elementary school there.

S: Where did you go after that?

G: Well, after Munich we lived in Saudi Arabia—we moved there when I was ten—then Alaska, and then Hawaii. In 2003, my father retired. Was it 2003? Yes…because I was 17.

S: Did you come to Los Angeles then?

G: No. My dad decided to retire in Hawaii. I didn't really like it there, so I applied to school in L.A.

S: So when did you come to Los Angeles?

G: Last year. Right after I finished high school. L.A. feels like my home now.

GIVE IT A TRY   **PAGE 85**

1. Discussing length of time

A: How long did you go to Pasadena High School?

B: I went there for four years.

2. Asking *What next?*

A: What did you do after high school?

B: I worked as a server for six weeks.

3. Describing changes

A: I used to hate cooking, but now I love it.

B: What made you change your mind?

A: It was when I tried vegetarian food.

LISTEN TO THIS   **PAGE 86**

Sting was born in Newcastle, England, on October 2, 1951. His father was a milkman. Sting's original name was Gordon Sumner. His friends called him Sting because he wore a yellow-and-black striped shirt that made him look like a bee.

He went to school in Newcastle and then went to university in Warwick. From 1971–1974 he attended a teacher training college. Afterward, he became a schoolteacher. He taught English, and played music in his free time. He didn't have much money.

Then he went to London. In 1977, he formed a rock group, The Police. They became a huge success. Their most famous song is "Every Breath You Take." Sting was a member of The Police until 1984 when he decided to go solo. In 1985, he started a jazz group called The Blue Turtles.

Now Sting is a millionaire with homes in Italy, England, and Malibu, California. He is very concerned about the environment and human rights. In 1989, he started the Rainforest Foundation to help save the rainforests in Brazil. In 2003, he wrote his autobiography, *Broken Music*.

Unit 11

GIVE IT A TRY   PAGE 89

1. Asking about past experiences

A: Have you ever gone to a foreign country?
B: Yes, several times.

2. Asking for a description or opinion

A: What do you think of Tokyo?
B: It's very big and exciting, but it's crowded.
A: What is the weather like?
B: It's really hot and humid.

3. Asking for more details

A: Have you ever been to New York?
B: Yes, I've been there several times.
A: What are the restaurants like?
B: They're pretty expensive.

LISTEN TO THIS   PAGE 90

L: Minako! How was your trip? I'm dying to hear all about it.
M: It was fantastic, Lynn. I loved it.
L: So, what did you think of San Francisco?
M: Beautiful. Have you ever been there?
L: No, I haven't, but I've always wanted to go. Tell me all about it.
M: Hmm. Where do I start? It really is a wonderful city. Mostly because it's so different. Everywhere you look there are hilly streets, beautiful old Victorian homes and buildings, the bay, and of course the Golden Gate Bridge.
L: Was it easy to get around?
M: Oh, yeah. I walked a lot, but when I got tired it was easy to get a bus. The bus system is really efficient and inexpensive, but the buses are a bit run-down. I also took the subway a couple of times. It was cheap, fast, and comfortable.
L: How about the cable cars?
M: They were always packed with people, but they were fun to ride.
L: What were the restaurants like?
M: There's a real variety. We had seafood at Fisherman's Wharf. It was really fresh and delicious, but it was kind of expensive. And we went to Chinatown for dinner one night. The food there was really spicy, but good.
L: How was your hotel?
M: It was small and very old. I felt like I was in an old movie! It wasn't fancy at all, but it was clean and well-kept, and the rates were reasonable.
L: Sounds wonderful. San Francisco, here I come.

GIVE IT A TRY   PAGE 93

1. Comparing places (1)

A: Which city do you like better, Montreal or Ottawa?
B: I think Ottawa is prettier, but Montreal is more exciting.

2. Comparing places (2)

A: Which place has nicer weather?
B: My hometown has nicer weather. It's always warm and sunny.

3. Comparing places (3)

A: Which city is the most exciting?
B: Montreal is the most exciting city in Canada.
A: Which city has the best scenery?
B: Vancouver. It has the most beautiful scenery in Canada.

LISTEN TO THIS   PAGE 94

D: Fran, you've been to Thailand, haven't you? How was it there? Did you like it?
F: Yes. I had a fantastic time! Why?
D: I'm planning a trip there in the summer. What are the best places to visit?
F: How long are you going for?
D: Oh, just for ten days. We're flying to Bangkok first. I thought we might stay there a few days.
F: Bangkok has really good restaurants, and there's quite a bit of sight-seeing too…. The Royal Palace, the temples…but the hotels aren't cheap. It's cheaper to stay outside the capital, somewhere like Chiang Mai or Phuket.
D: Which place did you like better, Chiang Mai or Phuket?
F: Well, both places are quite touristy. Chiang Mai is for more adventurous types. You can go trekking in the jungle, ride an elephant, or learn meditation at one of the ancient temples. It's quieter and more peaceful. You can stay in these really old-fashioned wooden houses. Phuket is more lively, there are more new hotels, and the nightlife is really good, though it can get noisy.
D: What are the people like?
F: People are really friendly everywhere in Thailand. But probably they are friendlier in a place like Chiang Mai, because it's smaller and less commercial.
D: What about the food?
F: It's fantastic! There are really good street restaurants everywhere you go. Be careful, it can be very spicy! In Chiang Mai, you get these delicious sour sauces and soups, and I loved the green papaya salad.
D: How about shopping? I want to get gifts for all my family.
F: It's great for shopping. You can get batik and silk at fabulous prices. Bangkok has the best shopping, because you get more choice, but the prices are higher there.
D: That's really helpful, thanks a lot! By the way, what's the weather like in August?
F: Very hot and humid! You'll need a hat for the sun, sunglasses, and plenty of sunscreen.

Unit 12

GIVE IT A TRY   PAGE 97

1. Discussing future plans (1)

A: What do you plan to do after you graduate?
B: I'm going to get a job right away.

2. Discussing future plans (2)

A: What are you going to do after you graduate?
B: I'm going to get a job right away.
A: What are you doing after that?
B: I'm going back to school.

3. Discussing future plans (3)

A: When will you be in Europe?
B: I'll be there on June 17.
A: How long will you be there?
B: I'll be there for six months.
A: What countries will you visit?
B: France and Italy.
A: What will you do there?
B: I'm going to learn about European art.

LISTEN TO THIS   PAGE 98

M: Well, Irene. Thank you for booking your tour with us. I'm sure you'll be very happy with the itinerary we have prepared for you. You'll see all the wonderful sights of Egypt in just six days!
I: Could you tell me a bit more about the details of the tour?
M: Yes, of course. You'll arrive in Cairo on Monday morning. It's an overnight flight, with a stopover in Athens. Hopefully, you'll be able to sleep on the plane, but just in case you are feeling tired, we've left Monday free for you to explore this exciting and exotic capital city.
I: Yes, I'm sure there'll be a lot to see.
M: Then on Tuesday you'll have a tour of the Pyramids at Giza and the Sphinx. Our expert guide will tell you all about the history of the ancient temples, tombs, and Pyramids. There's also an optional camel ride.
I: I think I'll skip that! Then we take the train to Aswan?
M: That's right, you'll arrive on Wednesday morning, and the same day you'll have the choice of a short river trip in a felucca, which is a traditional Egyptian type of river boat….
I: That sounds beautiful!
M: Or an optional tour to Abu Simbel. That's the famous temple high up above the Aswan dam. It takes about three hours by helicopter and it's one of the most spectacular sights in Egypt.
I: I'm not too sure about the helicopter— perhaps I'll leave that for next time.
M: Then you'll go on to Luxor by train. On Thursday you'll explore the Valley of the Kings. And Friday's tour of the Temple of

Karnak is an experience you will never forget!

I: Two days doesn't sound long enough. Will there be time for more sight-seeing when we get back to Cairo?

M: Yes, you'll have a whole afternoon free before your evening departure. There's a free tour of the Egyptian Museum, if you want, or you can go shopping…whatever you like.

I: It sounds fantastic! I can't wait!

GIVE IT A TRY   PAGE 101

1. Discussing goals

A: What do you want to do?

B: I want to study languages.

A: That sounds interesting. Which languages do you want to study?

B: I'd like to learn French and Spanish.

2. Discussing hopes

A: What do you hope you'll do next year?

B: I hope to get a job.

3. Discussing possibilities

A: What do you think you'll do after you graduate?

B: I might take some time off.

LISTEN TO THIS   PAGE 102

A: So what kind of job do you think you'll have in ten years, Ivan?

I: I'm not sure…. Something creative, I hope. I hope I'll be a musician or an artist. How about you?

A: Me, too. But perhaps I'll just end up working in an office and playing music in my spare time!

I: Where do you want to live? Do you think you'll stay in your hometown?

A: Yes, I like it there. In ten years I think I'll be married, with a home, and children….

I: Sounds good, Alexi…but I don't think I'll be settled down by then. I need more time to find my way in life. I might live abroad for a while…I definitely want to travel and see other countries like India and Australia….

A: I want to travel, but I'll always come back here, because this is where my friends are. I think it's difficult to make new friends.

I: I make new friends all the time! Like now, my personality is so different from when I was a teenager, and my friends are different, too. I used to be so shy, and now I'm not. I like going out. I like meeting new people.

A: I think in ten years, I'll be just the same as I am now. I'll wear the same clothes, and I'll have the same friends. My hair might be grayer.

I: Family and friends are really important to me, too. But I like change. I like to try new things. I can't stay in one place. In ten years, who knows what I'll be like!

Review Unit 10

LISTEN TO THIS   PAGE 104

He was born in the village of Qunu (q-u-n-u) in South Africa on July 18, 1918. When he was young, he decided to become a lawyer and fight for the rights of black people. He went to the University College of Fort Hare from 1938–40. He was suspended because of his political activities there.

After that, he finished his BA degree by correspondence. He joined the African National Congress in 1942, when he was 24. The ANC was an organization fighting to help get justice for black people in South Africa. He started a law practice in Johannesburg, where he worked to help black people who were thrown out of their homes and off their land.

In 1962, he was sent to prison. He was kept in prison until his release on February 11, 1990, when black people in South Africa finally won the right to vote. During all his years in prison, he never stopped working for justice and freedom for black people in South Africa.

After his release, he became the first democratically elected State President of South Africa on May 10, 1994. He retired from public life in June 1999. In 1974, while he was in prison, he had secretly started writing his autobiography, and it was finally published in 1994. It is called *Long Walk to Freedom*. His name is…Nelson Mandela.

Review Unit 11

LISTEN TO THIS   PAGE 104

R: So how was your European tour? Tell me all about it!

S: It was amazing. We visited three capital cities, Prague, Vienna, and Budapest, and we spent three days in each place.

R: So which city did you like best?

S: That's a really tough question! I think I liked Prague the best. It has the most historic buildings and it's very peaceful compared to Vienna. Vienna is noisier and has more traffic.

R: But I bet the food in Vienna was good!

S: Right! I ate the most delicious chocolate cake I've ever had in my life! The food in Vienna was way better than in Budapest or Prague. On the other hand, the prices in Prague and Budapest are much cheaper. Hotels and food are very expensive in Vienna. But they do have the best cake shops.

R: What about the people, were they friendly?

S: Yes, they were very friendly and helpful everywhere. In Vienna and Prague more people speak English than in Budapest.

R: Which city has the best stores?

S: I think Prague has the best stores. You can find all kinds of beautiful antiques and crafts. And at affordable prices. In fact, I bought so much stuff, I had to buy another suitcase to bring it home.

Review Unit 12

LISTEN TO THIS   PAGE 105

B: You know what, Jill? You work too hard. Let's go and sit in the park.

J: I can't do that. I have to study. Final exams are next week.

B: But, Jill…You already know that you're going to go to Harvard University. What are you going to major in anyway?

J: I'm taking economics and law. How about you? Which school are you going to next year, Ben?

B: Actually, I'm taking a year off. I'm going to Africa to work on an environmental program. I'll go to college the year after that.

J: What do you want to study?

B: I'm not really sure. I'd like to study environmental studies or geology. So, do you want to work for a big company after college, or do you want to do something else?

J: I hope to get into law school after I finish at Harvard.

B: Wow. You sure are ambitious!

J: What kind of job do you want to have after college?

B: Something easy. I'd like to work nine to five. I guess you'll be a lawyer.

J: Uh-huh. I'd like to practice law for a few years, and then I hope to go into politics.

B: Well, I just hope to have a steady job and a nice family.

J: Really? I think my job will always come first for me. I'd like to be a senator one day, or perhaps even president!